INFJ: 33 Secrets From The Life of an INFJ

By Diana Jackson

Contents

Book I.   **1**

1. Prefers Dreaming to Real Life   2

2. Hatred of Crowds   5

3. Fear of Making a Mistake   8

4. Creativity   11

5. Organizational Skills   14

6. Anxiety   17

7. Crying   19

8. Demanding of Self   22

9. Worries   25

10. Enjoyment of Solitude   28

11. Frequent Daydreaming   31

12. Emotional Clinginess   34

13. A Tragic Sense of Life   37

14. Ease of being hurt   39

15. A Moody Demeanor   41

16. Perfectionist Traits   43

17. Loneliness   46

18. Idealization of a perfect relationship   49

19. Fear of Rejection   51

20. Dislike of Noise   54

21. Easily Distracted   56

22. Moved to Tears by Books or Movies   58

23. High Sensitivity to the Moods of Others   60

24. Easily Overwhelmed   63

25. Sensitive Skin   66

26. Enjoys Complexity   68

27. Likes to Analyze Patterns   71

28. Likes to Analyze Motivations of Others   74

29. Doesn't Like Too Much Attention   77

30. Cautious   80

31. Easily Frightened   82

32. Intelligent   85

33. Prone to Self-analysis   87

Book II.   **91**

1. Geoffrey Chaucer   93

2. Gillian Anderson   96

3. Cate Blanchett   99

4. Nelson Mandela   102

5. Martin Luther King, Jr.   105

6. Mother Teresa   107

7. Mahatma Gandhi   109

8. Eleanor Roosevelt   112

9. Carl Jung   115

10. Florence Nightingale   118

11. Jimmy Carter   121

12. Mary Wollstonecraft   124

13. Lady Gaga   127

Book I.

33 Secrets from Life of an INFJ.

INFJ: It stands for Introverted, Intuitive, Feeling, and Judging — a rare combination to which only a small percentage of the world's population can lay claim. While each and every personality on the MBTI spectrum has something unique to offer the world, INFJs are especially creative and compassionate, while also maintaining a cool, somewhat aloof reserve that makes it difficult for strangers to penetrate the deeper wellsprings of emotion and feeling that are toiling about within. If people only knew what the INFJ was thinking underneath that retiring façade! If only INFJs were more comfortable putting themselves out there! Yet these factors are what makes the INFJ such a joy to unravel and such a treasure to their friends.

Even their closest friends and relatives, however, can experience frustration when it comes to certain aspects of the INFJ personality, so strangers or casual acquaintances cannot be faulted for not having a whole lot of insight into the secretive, private INFJ. What some people might not realize is that on the surface only are these types shy, reserved, or even "unfriendly." And that is what this book hopes to highlight: 33 INFJ-specific traits, explained in full as they are applicable to all the areas in this personality's life. This book should help others understand this most unique and rare personality type, while giving INFJs the insight they need to strengthen their weaknesses and capitalize on their many strengths.

1. Prefers Dreaming to Real Life

Positive aspect: Who else but a dreamer imagines things that everyone else says can't be done? Who else pushes the boundaries of what is known to be possible? Creativity is one of the touchstones of this personality type, as are a yearning for new possibilities and the ability to think outside the established box. In fact, one of the greatest advocates for pushing through the accepted social norms was an INFJ: Martin Luther King, Jr. How's that for having a dream?

Negative aspect: Imagining an ideal situation or person is something we all do, but the INFJs will happily persist in their daily lives by functioning with a maddening preference for how they think things should be, and not how they really are. Picture a friend who fantasizes about becoming a famous writer and then turns up his nose at a perfectly good job in retail because it is "beneath" his self-perceived talents. It's enough to make you want to throttle that person! In the real world, you have to take what you can get, because fantasies lack tangible substance.

In Relationships: Idealizing a partner can work one of two ways: INFJs may either spend their entire lives trying to find the "dream girl" or "dream guy" who doesn't exist, or they could be happily blinded to their partner's faults. In the case of the latter, so long as it is a mutually adoring and respectful relationship, INFJs will often have stars in their eyes long after others' honeymoon periods have been spent. When it comes to the former, INFJs should be aware that their generous, Feeling natures can make them susceptible to manipulative people.

At Work: The INFJ brings an interesting personality dichotomy to the workplace with his/her daydreaming. Though they are given to fantasizing about winning Employee of the Year or getting a rightfully deserved bonus, it is the INFJs' imaginations that set them apart. They are creative, and not just in artistic fields; the sciences are always in need of professionals like the INFJ, who think and imagine beyond what is known and who can problem-solve in new, daring ways. What the INFJ dreams might not be real life yet, but it's only a matter of time before these motivated go-getters make it so.

With Friends: While friends might have to snap their fingers a few times to get the INFJ to come back down to earth, this personality's dreamy disposition works well for groups in other ways. INFJs' considerable imagination is perfect for coming up with harebrained schemes full of hilarity and fun, and their Judging aspect gives them the organizational skills to actually make it happen. Since INFJs, like most other Introverts, prefer having a close-knit group of friends, their propensity for dreaming up diversions only cements their fondness of their buddies.

Health: INFJs who may have put on a few pounds will spend tons of time either reminiscing about their younger, slimmer physiques, or picturing themselves after a year of hard work put in at the gym. It might stop there, but if the INFJ can just get him/herself to the gym, he/she has the dedication and ability to commit, as a Judging type, to get real results. The important thing is that INFJs find an activity they genuinely love, so that they don't slip back into just fantasizing about a healthier self.

Finances: Despite being well organized and willing to make commitments for the future, INFJs can lack a certain practicality that Sensing types bring to the table. Their Intuitive nature makes them dreamier and more attracted to the abstract, but finances are an area firmly rooted in the concrete, so INFJs must engage their Judging aspect and realize that if they want the free time to dream, they must put in the hard work and make the money that gives them space to fantasize.

2. Hatred of Crowds

Positive Aspect: A jostling crowd of people does not appeal to everyone, and the INFJ is certainly among that group. So consider: when was the last time you had a chance to get to know someone really well among a big crowd of people? Emotionally complex and deeply caring, INFJs' strong intuition guides them toward people with whom they sense they can create lasting bonds of friendship, and they take the time to get to know friends on a meaningful level. If the INFJ suggests at a party that you grab a coffee the next day, that is his/her way of saying, "This crowd makes me want to dash, but I really like you enough to see you again!"

Negative Aspect: Of course, an aversion to crowds may lead many to think that their INFJ friend is something like a hermit or a recluse, and those who don't know him/her well will only witness an inherent standoffishness and surmise that individual is a snob or unfriendly. The INFJ may be known as the wet blanket in his/her social circle, the one who bails on everyone early in the night or who brings down everyone else's fun during a night out. It's not intentional on INFJs' behalf — in fact, they are thinking everyone will have more fun if they aren't there complaining — but it can look like they hold themselves above the activity.

In Relationships: In romantic relationships, INFJs' dislike of crowds will likely dictate with whom they couple off. They will have an affinity for other Introverts like them, people who do not insist on wild nights out at the club (oh, horror!) and who appreciate a solid night in, cooking dinner and watching old movies — that is, connecting, on a more personal level. Family members probably won't find the issue too pressing – unless there's a big reunion coming up and the INFJ is rattling off a hundred reasons why he/she just can't make it.

At Work: Much like in their romantic relationships, this aspect of INFJs' personality will dictate where they work and/or how happy they are in their place of employment. It is unlikely you will see an INFJ as a party promoter or even a teacher, though INFJs do have the patience and nurturing spirit for it; instead, expect the INFJ to be happiest in more personal, one-on-one kinds of service-oriented careers, like counseling or therapy, or — even better — simply working for him/herself as a writer or artist.

With Friends: Some INFJs with Extraverted friends might make the effort more often to go out and be among a young, pulsing crowd of people, but it is likely that they are thinking, wistfully, of the earliest exit strategy they can come up with ("Have I used the 'feed the cat' line already?"). Instead of giving in and doing something that makes them uncomfortable, INFJs can instead reach out by offering to organize a smaller get-together of just their closest pals at a winery or even in their own home.

Health: If INFJs forces themselves to hang out among crowds, whether in their social lives or at work, they could end up the worse for it health-wise. Repeated exposure to a situation that makes them uncomfortable is likely to make them irritable, but more significantly, it can lead to elevated levels of stress, which are linked to numerous health issues involving the heart. No

INFJ should put his or her heart health at risk for a career he/she hates or friends who, if they are true friends, understand that the INFJ just wants to stay home.

Finances: INFJs' dislike of crowds can affect their finances in a few ways. First, it can compel them to seek certain kinds of jobs — namely ones where they are left to their own devices and there is not a lot of teamwork involved. Entrepreneurship is an attractive venture, though it does create a money vacuum that can be difficult to close, especially if the business doesn't get off the ground. Second, INFJs aren't likely to find themselves regularly buying rounds of drinks for their 100 closest friends.

3. Fear of Making a Mistake

Positive: The INFJ is a perfectionist, make no mistake – a trait that will influence how he/she responds to every given task. INFJs' goals might not qualify as exceedingly ambitious (no ruthless CEOs here), but what they do pursue, whether it's a career, hobbies, or personal aspirations, will be done to the best of their ability and with perfection in mind. This makes them reliable, trustworthy, and capable individuals, and ensures that the quality of what they do is always top-notch.

Negative: You try carrying the weight of so much perfection on your shoulders and see if that doesn't leave you drained at the end of each day. No one is exempt from making a mistake now and then, and the infamously Intuitive INFJ, who truly believes that his/her way is the best, could end up collapsing under the disappointment and guilt. It's a very difficult way to go through life, and it is difficult for others to relate.

In relationships: Not wanting to hurt their partners by doing or saying the wrong thing, INFJs are a model of tact and graciousness in a relationship. But even with their sincerely compassionate nature, it takes a special person to stick around long enough to peel away INFJs' deeper layers. Attentive and affectionate as parents, those of this personality type are also the kind to stress so hard over which stroller to buy that they have a stroke. A good match for INFJs is, surprisingly, a logical Thinker, someone who can pull them out of their own head and ground them with reality when necessary.

At Work: Perfectionism in the workplace is a boon, and INFJs will always have their work completed on time, signed, sealed, and delivered with a bow; not only that, but their work will also be of the highest possible quality. Chances are, they will view their own work with the most scrutiny and criticism, far more than any boss. The only drawback to this fear of mistakes is that coworkers may harbor resentments and competitiveness, maybe even making the sensitive INFJ the butt of some snarky jokes.

With Friends: Aside from their romantic partners, friends are an important influence on the INFJ, who needs to be saved from him/herself once a while. While the INFJ is not the personality who critiques friends for being less-than-perfect, those of this type are hard on themselves and fear making mistakes in their own lives. But seeing a friend make mistakes and yet survive can prove to be an excellent example for INFJs, allowing them to feel comfortable trying something new without their usual fear of failure.

Health: Like other Introverts, INFJs are at risk for high levels of stress because of what's going on in their heads (unlike Extraverts, who tend to burn out because they are involved with too many people and projects). The constant self-nagging, as well as the inner voice that pushes them harder to do better and be more, are hallmarks of this perfectionist personality type, sometimes to their own detriment. INFJs have to learn how to calm down, accept "flaws" or "weaknesses," and accept themselves for who they are.

Finances: INFJs who amass a hefty sum by the time they are ready to retire may fall into the category of "having saved so much all their lives that now they are afraid to spend." A good financial advisor will tell them, yes, it's okay to finally make some stupid purchases and maybe buy yourself that boat you've been dreaming of. INFJ, take this money professional at his/her word; you lived financially mistake-free your entire life — now it's time to have fun! There are no mistakes, no matter how luxurious the object, as long as you can afford the purchase.

4. Creativity

Positive: There is no limit to the positive attributes possible because of INFJs' infinite capacity for creativity. They are always pushing boundaries, solving problems in new and exciting ways, and inspiring others to do the same. Look at the INFJs who have walked the earth: Nelson Mandela, Mother Theresa, and Jerry Seinfeld are just a few. All three broke new ground in their respective fields and influenced thousands, perhaps even millions of their followers because they chose a different path than the ones already forged.

Negative: Such abundant and vibrant energy from INFJs can make them individuals who are difficult to contain in social and work situations. Their boundless creativity may make them feel stifled or bored among "regular" people who lack their insight and freethinking, and as a result they can be or feel alienated, which is further impacted by their dislike of crowds to begin with. They may also scandalize or insult people with their more avant-garde approach to life.

In Relationships: INFJs creativity makes them fun partners and fun parents, the sort to come up with zany, unique date nights or great games for family night. Their ability to think outside of the box means that no problem in the home is beyond their solving (whether it's the bathroom's leaky pipe or a daughter's recent breakup), and they often encourage others in their immediate family to think likewise, nurturing ideas in a judgment-free space while encouraging detail-oriented activities.

At Work: Thanks to their excess of creativity, INFJs often finds themselves in artistic fields like writing or painting. Yet their strong Intuition, which informs this part of their personality, also makes them the kind of people who do well in the sciences, where hunches and gut feelings have led to some pretty incredible discoveries. The superior problem-solving, which comes from a keen creativity, also makes them good counselors and therapists, as well as able administrators; in fact, INFJs would make terrific personal assistants and receptionists.

With Friends: If their friends didn't already love them for their generous and kind natures, they would adore them anyways for the quickness of mind that is the product of INFJs' creativity. INFJs might not care to engage in big group discussions, but among their close friends and family, they are great fun to talk to, bringing clever humor, wit, and even a surprising dose of sass to the conversation. Puns, inside jokes with longevity and astute, whip-smart assessments of others are INFJs' bread and butter.

Health: Because their creative natures are a result of their innate open-mindedness, INFJs are willing to explore all types of healthcare options, including traditional medicines as well as natural and homeopathic remedies. In fact, INFJs gain a great deal of satisfaction from resolving minor health issues through DIY methods, like cayenne pepper tea for a sore throat or special homemade scrubs to improve dry skin. INFJs certainly value accredited medical professionals, but they are equally open to the healing possibilities of the natural world.

Finances: Getting creative with one's financial situation might sound like a terrifying prospect to a firmly Sensing type, but for the INFJ, it's part and parcel of living a creative life, and this personality type is undaunted by the prospect of cobbling together a living with a few different sources of income. Further, INFJs have all the makings of coupon-clipping queens and kings; they are the types who can eventually go grocery shopping and only pay a few dollars for an entire cart of food.

5. Organizational Skills

Positive: While it is true that some INFJs will be messier, they will sometimes veer toward the other end of the spectrum and become intensely detail-oriented, making them very organized and precise. A well-ordered INFJ may enjoy a more compartmentalized existence that helps this personality type manage free-flowing and liberal tendencies, such as daydreaming. Far from putting a stopper on their creativity, strong organizational skills work in concert with INFJs' natural tendencies for a more productive individual.

Negative: The drawbacks of an INFJ who naturally rejects organization are obvious, but more interesting are the negative aspects for one who does have a strong sense of it. It is not uncommon for the patently introverted INFJs to become so wholly immersed in the minor aspects of something that they fail to see the whole picture. And unfortunately, when others don't live up to their organizational standards, they can be critical, further shutting out people than this Introverted type already tends to do.

In Relationships: Picture the earnest INFJ planning a beautiful and special anniversary trip to Hawaii, but getting so worked up over choosing the most centrally located hotel for sightseeing that he/she mistakenly makes the reservations for the wrong month. Still, INFJs always want the best for their partners and families, and will use their ample organizational skills to give that to them. These skills also help the INFJ to manage hectic family lives, though with a surprisingly amount of flexibility so that one surprise meeting or soccer game can be absorbed with minor fuss.

At Work: Even the organized INFJ might not have the neatest work space, but desks and drawers aren't the only things that require detailed attention. Ideas are the lifeblood of INFJs, and they have both the creativity to come up with some great ones and the drive to see them through. Of course, ideas can only turn into reality thanks to precise and deliberate actions, and the comprehensive mind of an INFJ will rise to that challenge on the job. Though INFJs don't prefer to be large and in charge, they prove themselves to be capable managers of both people and events.

With Friends: If your group of friends needs someone to book the plane tickets and map out a rough sketch of the daily activities before you take your vacation, hit up the INFJ of the clique and ask if he/she can get the wheels in motion. INFJs are not only useful in situations where planning is needed, they truly enjoy doing it, as it gives them a sense of control, productivity, and even happiness — happiness that they are contributing to the happiness of others!

Health: Unlike their INFP counterparts, when the INFJ makes a doctor's appointment, you can bet he/she will be there — on time, if not a little bit early. This isn't to say that INFJs don't suffer from the same types of nervousness that everyone else does when it comes to the idea of sitting on that examination table and being poked and prodded; rather, INFJs are resolved to do what they must to maintain good physical order.

Finances: INFJs might be dreamers and idealists, but they will have a firm grasp of their financial situation because their Judging aspect gives them a natural affinity for keeping an eye on the small details and managing their affairs with an air of responsibility. The INFJ who dreams of one day buying an expensive motorcycle is likely to create an organized savings plan, spend years building a little fortune, and then live to ride with the additional satisfaction of a person who made good on a personal goal.

6. Anxiety

Positive: Anxiety – how is this a good thing? You might be surprised when it comes to the INFJ, whose anxious feelings and thoughts are most commonly the result of an almost supernatural intuition that informs how this type behaves. If INFJs are agitated about something, then it is almost certainly with good reason, and they are less likely to act (or react) without a great deal of careful observation, their anxiousness serving them as a call for thorough examination.

Negative: Yet a constant state of anxiety, always lurking under the surface because it is such an integral part of their personality, can be very damaging to the INFJ's emotional and psychological health. Panic attacks and anxiety attacks may render the necessity for medication, and the stress can take its toll on both the INFJ's mind and appearance. And of course, those around this personality type may reach the point where they say, "Enough. You need to calm down." Which they probably do!

In Relationships: One of the sweetest ways a partner can show his/her love is by expressing worry and care. INFJs love rarely and deeply, and they will be anxious not only for reciprocating love, but for the welfare of their chosen partner and family. Children of an INFJ may find themselves always at the mercy of their parent's strong intuition, but that worry is always tempered with a sincere and heartfelt love.

At Work: Anxiety might make INFJs basket cases during a job interview, piles of nerves as they wait to receive their performance review, and total nuts when people in their company are being let go. INFJs should always try to separate their work lives from their home lives, or the stress may take its toll in negative ways. But for those who pursue service-oriented jobs, the anxious concern they show is for those they are trying to help and better.

With Friends: Friends can have a soothing influence on anxious INFJs, so it is important that those of this personality type let themselves be helped by others and reach out when they feel like their insides are going to burst. Just having someone to talk to can be enough, but even better is having a friend who can help them see things from an objective perspective — which is, more often than not, a much better way of looking at things than what is going on in the INFJ's head.

Health: If the INFJ can come up with effective ways of dealing with anxiety, so much the better — it's not going anywhere anytime soon, and a proactive way of handling it is the best course of action. Some INFJs might veer into a different territory, however, one in which their anxiety becomes crippling and life altering. Most INFJs, who have a strong sense of self, will recognize that they need help, or will, with any luck, be open to the concerns of friends and family.

Finances: Even though INFJs are quite good at managing their money and spending responsibly, it still won't stop them from worrying about whether or not they have enough. INFJs who have families to support will feel the weight of their anxiety in this area, but they can easily offset this by keeping a savings nest egg, equivalent to the amount of six months' pay (the typical period of time during which unemployment compensation can be collected). Having a safety net should alleviate most financial worries.

7. Crying

Positive: Well, there's no mistaking when an INFJ has been moved to his/her core, because this personality type will cry easily. Yet it's not just a matter of sad things happening; often, those tears are tears of joy, as they can think of no better way to show their extreme sensitivity to the happiness of those around them by blubbering a bit. Let's face it: a special event like a wedding isn't complete without the female INFJ weeping off her mascara, and no one shows his sensitive side like the male INFJ, who is touched to his core by a good book.

Negative: On the other hand, sometimes you may want your INFJ friend to put in a sock in it. Having someone seemingly melt under pressure or stress can be the very last thing anyone needs, particularly in times of crisis when calm is your ally. Yet the INFJ cannot help him/herself, and the crying will always be an issue, no matter how much you wish it otherwise. Prepare yourself for a lifetime of carrying tissues, because these Feeling types might start sniffling during one of those awful rescue-pet commercials.

In Relationships: Sweet or startling, particularly in male INFJs, make no mistake that what seem like easy tears in a relationship actually come out only when those of this personality type have found their perfect match. They are lovers who will cherish every moment with their mate as special and significant, often leaking from the eyes with the power of their emotion. And children of an INFJ, prepare yourselves: Mom and/or Dad will be the one crying at the dance recital (and hopefully capturing it all on the running video they took, so that it can be giggled over in the future).

At Work: Ultrasensitive to critique and determined to slide away from conflict, when faced with either, the INFJ may be found alone in the stall of the workplace bathroom, trying to cry quietly so as not to disturb his/her coworkers. It might seem extreme to everyone else who holds it together and presses onward, but this is just how INFJs gets their wellspring of emotion out. Never underestimate that rejuvenating feeling after a good hard cry, and keep tissues close about because you don't know when your eyes will start to leak.

With Friends: Is there anything more precious than the INFJ's barely holding it together during the sappy movie you made her go see? Or the sweetness of the male INFJ blubbering over a cute puppy at the rescue shelter? If nothing else, INFJs make their less weepy friends feel quite stoic in comparison, but it is equally beneficial if they get their friends crying, too — again, shedding tears is wonderfully cathartic!

Health: How cathartic? Crying not only alleviates sadness and anger, it can lessen stress, remove toxins from your body, and help keep your eyes comfortably lubricated. So bring on the tear-jerker movies, the sappy Facebook posts about random strangers doing good things out of the blue, even the breakups that are for the best, yet still hurt — crying is human, and INFJs are great humans who deserve a satisfying sob now and then.

Finances: Getting their credit card bill at the end of each month makes most people want to cry, but INFJs are perfectly comfortable actually letting those tears roll down their cheeks (if, say, they had a momentary and drunken lapse in judgment and did some online shopping). Such is the rejuvenating effect of crying, though, that INFJs can have their little pity party and then get on with their lives, feeling much better and even more resolved to continue their streak of financial responsibility.

8. Demanding of Self

Positive: One of the most unique things about INFJs is how much they will dare to dream and how far they will push themselves to go to realize their ideals. Their parents may have simply wanted them to go to college, but they one-upped them by getting into Harvard. These personality types are extremely self-motivated and dare themselves to accomplish much, making them some of the most powerful movers and shakers in this world — look at Gandhi, who championed Indian liberation from the British Empire, and former President Jimmy Carter, who became leader of the free world after being a peanut farmer.

Negative: All that self-determination can, however, come crashing down if those goals they have set for themselves do not come to fruition. INFJs may deride themselves excessively for not living up to their own lofty personal standards, a personality tic which can be difficult to watch and even harder to remedy by those around them. Nobody is perfect, but don't tell INFJs that, because they would like to prove you wrong, to their own stubborn detriment.

In Relationships: Being in a relationship with the INFJ is not for everyone, and this is one of the most glaring examples why: while INFJs are determined individuals who will always be sensitive to your needs, if they feel they have failed you, you could end up dealing with a self-flagellating lover who has to be coaxed out of their very real, but frustratingly pervasive guilt when they feel as though they have wronged you in some way or failed to hold up their end of the bargain. It might be brutal, but telling them to quit being a martyr is one avenue for snapping them out of it.

At Work: It is very rare for a boss to tell his/her employee that they should "Ease up on themselves," but this may be the case for the INFJ worker, whose visions and dreams consistently push him/her to attain the very heights of ambition. Often the INFJ will choose a career that lets him/her pursue personal goals and ideals, like jobs in social work that better society by helping individuals. INFJs' instinctive passion for making a difference pushes them to demand much of themselves no matter what they do, though, even if it's flipping burgers as a teenager.

With Friends: Along with their significant other, INFJs' friends can offer a great deal of support and reassurance — reassurance that the INFJ is enough without having to be perfect or to be considered the very best at something. Support, too, if/when the INFJ fails to meet his or her lofty goals, like a dream job that he/she didn't get or coming in with a longer time than expected at a marathon. INFJs aren't as needy as their INFP "cousins," but they need to hear encouragement as much as anyone.

Health: INFJs aren't likely to suffer injuries from extreme sports, but rather, extreme stress. Because they hope to be the very cream of the crop when it comes to all aspects of their life, the pressure they put on themselves is immense — so much so, that some INFJs bend under the circumstances, while others break entirely. Lack of sleep or poor quality of sleep, a bad diet, and not getting enough leisure time to do things they enjoy can make INFJs irritable and emotionally unstable.

Finances: INFPs don't give a hoot about earning enough to buy a private jet, and while INFJs aren't setting out to become the next Donald Trump either, they have a more motivated sense of financial responsibility, thanks to their Judging aspect. Whereas some types might be okay with letting their parents continue to foot the bill into their adult years, from the time the INFJ turned 18, he or she made a point of becoming financially independent and able to buy all of his/her own things.

9. Worries

Positive: Like a sensitive, concerned mother, the naturally nurturing INFJ is almost always worried about something and someone. This sincere level of care and concern for others means that those who know the INFJ also know they can count on that person, no matter what, and know that the INFJ's prayers and thoughts are always with them, sending out positive vibes into the universe. Sometimes, all we really need is to know that someone cares or is sitting at home worrying for us.

Negative: Anyone who worries too much is probably also overthinking, and that can get bothersome for both the individual and those around him/her. Sometimes, the INFJ needs to be told to just calm down and put his/her worries out of mind because – as is so often the case in the human experience – there is just nothing to be done, and the INFJ's worrying can only make situations worse. Of course, that's like trying to talk a determined man away from a tall building ledge. INFJs need to learn to balance their Feeling aspects with Thinking qualities, where logic and reason have their say.

In Relationships: When you don't get that job promotion or suddenly find your relationship with your mother floundering, the INFJ is there, concerned, every step of the way. This is both comforting and a bit overwhelming, especially if the INFJ's concern starts to intensify until it is stronger than yours. And ask any child of an INFJ if he/she would use the word "overbearing" to describe the INFJ parent – the child might say that's putting it mildly. Yet the INFJ is, if nothing else, a motivated and involved significant other and parent.

25

At Work: The workplace is a source of worry for most people who don't even have the particular depth of feeling that an INFJ experiences, so imagine how much more difficult it can be for someone who is constantly informed by intuition – which is almost always right. INFJs' worrying does often push them to perform to the best of their abilities, but it can add to the stress that ravages their bodies and minds.

With Friends: Again, friends of INFJs can come to appreciate the fact that someone is looking out for and worrying about them. It's a bit sweet when the INFJ says, "Text me when you get home so I know you're safe." But, the worrying can also put a damper on fun, such as when the whole group of college buddies wants to take a spontaneous trip to Vegas, but the INFJ pumps the breaks and says, "Wait! What about our jobs? What will our wives say?"

Health: There is no denying that excessive worry can have a negative effect on the body, especially when the anxiety is permeating. But there are also cases where INFJs' propensity for freaking out is a good thing for their health, like when they spot a suspicious mole or experience flu-like symptoms that feel just slightly off. Striking the right balance between silly, excessive fear and informed worrying is a tall order, but the INFJ is eminently capable.

Finances: It's a bit ironic that INFJs worry about money, because they are usually so good about managing it. This isn't the type to make impulsive splurges on expensive clothes or new cars, yet the normal issues of the rent being raised, a sudden expense if their laptop dies, or even a big event like a wedding or the beginning of the school year can make the

INFJs' blood pressure rise. The important thing for this organized type is to plan well ahead, so that the worrying is reduced overall.

10. **Enjoyment of Solitude**

Positive: When Henry David Thoreau withdrew from the bustle of 19th-century life in New England, he ended up using his time of reflection to pen one of the most beloved and influential works of American nonfiction, *Walden Pond*. Clearly there is something special to the enjoyment of solitude, and the naturally introverted INFJs know and appreciate it. It is a time for them to recharge and to refocus, something many of us forget to do, to our own detriment. INFJs in particular might use this time for creative good, allowing them the time and space to bring something truly breathtaking into the world, be it a poem, sculpture, or scientific theory.

Negative: Of course, wanting to be alone in peace and quiet can be very inconvenient if the INFJ is needed elsewhere. And because they are such friendly, thoughtful people, others want to be around INFJs, enjoying their company, and may be hurt or confused by the INFJS' social withdrawal. Even if you understand why the INFJ simply does not want to present as a keynote speaker at your event, it's still disappointing and feels like a rebuff. INFJs must be sensitive to those who could feel excessively slighted or they will end up burning bridges.

In Relationships: INFJs who have coupled off will innately understand one another's desire to be alone, but other personality types might have a more difficult time accepting it. Indeed, it can lead to tension in relationships, especially when you have given your heart to someone and come to find that he/she suddenly needs to block out everyone – including you. Know that this aspect is simply part of the INFJ personality and not a personal attack on the way you smell.

At Work: Didn't everyone pretty much hate working on group projects in high school or college? These tasks were especially painful for the INFJ, who works best in low-to-no crowd careers – such as a research scientist who performs most of his/her work independently or a freelance writer who can complete his/her latest novel at a coffee shop, headphones on, everyone else tuned out. Don't expect to find too many INFJ personalities in retail if they can help it.

With Friends: It's good for INFJs to have an Extraverted friend or two to finally pull them out of their determined solitude, but for the most part, friends should learn to let their INFJ pals go it alone for a few days. It's a good opportunity for those of this personality type to reclaim their spent energy, then come back to the people they care about with a genuine enthusiasm for company and zest for life. When they do rejoin their pals, they are ready as ever with laughter, jokes, and witty conversation, so much so that they might even feel like the life of the party.

Health: INFJs should take advantage of their solitude by doing the things they love, whether it's reading, writing, kayaking on an open lake, or taking themselves out to a matinee. It is important for people to learn how to do things alone (or just be alone) with only their own thoughts for company. For INFJs, voluntary solitude is something that makes them happy, and that happiness improves their quality of life and overall health.

Finances: INFJs' enjoyment of solitude can be good for their finances in a few different ways. First, it allows them time to set their financial goals and think about new ways to meet them, like what kind of costs they can cut throughout their month to sock more away into savings. Second, if the INFJ is alone, it's a good chance he/she is not spending much money, as hanging out with friends tends to lead to little expenses that add up.

11. Frequent Daydreaming

Positive: There is nothing like an INFJ lost in thought, because you know he/she has gone down the rabbit hole and is having some pretty fantastical thoughts. But "fantastical" and "applicable" aren't necessarily mutually exclusive — and that's what is so forgivable in those of this type of personality (that may not be so in others): the assurance that whatever they are dreaming, it is something big, and it is also most likely something that will help others, because that is what the INFJ is known for doing.

Negative: Of course, those bouts of daydreaming can get a bit excessive from an outsider's perspective, especially when there are things that need to be done. In addition, while the INFJ is frequently known and respected grand achievements, who knows what opportunities he/she missed because his/her head was so frequently floating up in the clouds, with nary a concern for the realities of life.

In Relationships: The dreamer is passionate and imaginative in relationships, and the partner of an INFJ can rest assured that those frequent daydreams involve love. Yet while it is nice to know that we are being thought of through the flattering tint of rose-colored glasses, the reality of relationships is that they take work – real, actual work – to thrive and survive. Luckily, the INFJ can back up his/her constant bouts of fantasizing with creative solutions for fixing relationship problems.

At Work: Thanks to that same flair for creativity, INFJs may get a pass at work on occasion for being such daydreamers at their desks, because they are very often the ones who come through with the big idea or the innovative new way to fix an old problem. Yet their chin-in-hand repose may come off as impossibly lazy to coworkers, who have been chugging energy drinks since 7 a.m. to stay focused. INFJs also run the risk of little productivity if they work from home, yet in their living room/office, at least no one can get irritated by the frequency with which their minds wander.

With Friends: Getting INFJs to rejoin everyone in the real world can be a challenge, but their friends are probably used to it — and might even just let their INFJ friends stay there a little while, with that dreamy, blank expression on their faces. Even better, though, friends of INFJs can tap into their expansive talent for imagining things and have them come up with some innovative solutions for whatever is ailing them. Just set them to the task and let them work it out with those fiercely intelligent brains.

Health: As long as INFJs don't drive off a cliff because they were too busy daydreaming about winning a Nobel Peace Prize, their daytime fantasies shouldn't prove to be much of a health issue. In fact, if there's any effect, it's most likely positive, as escapism keeps INFJs calm and happy, a welcome respite from the usual worry and anxiety that can overwhelm their senses. In fact, daydreams are a definite improvement over worries, and could even be used as a type of soothing meditation.

Finances: Daydreams can be a powerful tool for the INFJs, who are usually quite good at managing their money. Unlike Perceiving types, who have the spontaneity in their personality to just go ahead and buy the thing they're drooling over (price be damned!), INFJs will imagine themselves on the boat or riding the bike, and feel even more determined to save toward that goal.

12. Emotional Clinginess

Positive: Emotional clinginess might not be for everyone, but those who like to feel important and needed will get a real kick out of INFJs' suction cup-like devotion. In a world where we are taught to be emotional islands, self-sufficient and independent, it is a welcome change to be needed and to let ourselves be needed by those who can benefit from our own wellspring of personal strength.

Negative: Yet emotional clinginess can quickly sour, and those to whom the INFJ has fastened him/herself may find that they are drained, with nothing else emotionally for anyone else in their lives. While it is a precious few to whom the INFJ personality forms strong bonds of friendship, those privileged enough to be invited into the INFJ's inner sanctum may find themselves exhausted by the effort needed to sustain the partnership.

In Relationships: If INFJs are picky about their friends, then they are downright persnickety when choosing romantic mates; as a result, they may form intense attachments to their lovers once an appropriate one has been found. This can either be thrilling or terrifying, depending on the individual, and in some cases it may be a mixture of both. However, when you find yourself on the receiving end of an INFJ's neediness, tread lightly if you don't exactly reciprocate. The worst things you can do to an INFJ are to fake your interest and waste their time.

At Work: Because INFJs don't get close to just anyone, should they be in a career in which they work with or around others, then any coworker with whom they form a friendship has a

34

comrade for life, in or out of work. But this also means that said coworker will need patience and a naturally caring disposition, because INFJs may require some comforting when they stress out to the point of breakdown or receive sharp critique from the boss. The coworker can expect marathon email conversations or texts throughout the workday!

With Friends: INFJs feel a special kinship with the friends who experience emotion the same way they do (freely, that is, thanks to their Feeling aspect), so it is no surprise that these types share clinginess with their closest confidantes. Yet "clingy" certainly has negative connotations, and what INFJs share with their most treasured friends is a transcendent understanding that they will be there for each other, no matter what. INFJs might command the loyalty of their pals, but it's nothing short of what they give out in kind.

Health: Emotional clinginess can veer in an unhealthy direction, however, especially if the INFJ starts turning to others to prop up his/her self-esteem or self-worth. Should INFJs find themselves at the mercy of others' opinions or affection, they could develop a cult-like obsession with that person (or those people), always seeking affirmation or validity for themselves, rather than developing their own personal sense of self-confidence.

Finances: Though INFJs' emotional clinginess shouldn't have much bearing on how they spend or save their money, this part of their personality could come to bear on how often others try to hit them up for a "loan." They might feel as though they "owe" something to someone for always being there when they are in a bad way emotionally. But the fact is, money and friendships (or familial relationships) rarely mix. Consider well before lending money to someone and be aware of the fact that this person could be using emotional clinginess against you.

13. A Tragic Sense of Life

Positive: When tragedy strikes the INFJ, this most deeply affected of all the personalities takes it to heart for the rest of his/her life. The positive in this is that, through tragedy, we gain a sharper understanding of who we are and oftentimes grow in emotional strength by triumphing over the sadness that has touched our lives. INFJs always remember, and it helps to inform their compassionate, empathic nature, which in turn inspires the same in others.

Negative: The danger in going through life with such a strong sense of the tragic is that it is easy to be overwhelmed by it and consumed by the darkness. It is easy to start looking at every sad event as yet another example of the world's evil, even when there is yet so much good. Because of the INFJs' limitless capacity for emotional depth, it may be difficult for them to pull back from the darkness, which can lead to psychological disorders.

In Relationships: One thing is for certain: if the INFJ has experienced tragedy in his/her own life, it may take months, and even years, for that person's partner to get it out of him/her because of INFJs' natural trepidation for really opening up to someone. If the INFJ's mate is intuitive, he/she will sense the sadness or see it in his/her partner's eyes. For some, that is powerfully attractive. Just beware of letting the INFJ lover wallow in that misery.

At Work: INFJs are probably the first people to take a personal day when they are too emotionally distraught to come to work. It could be something as serious as a death in the family or as distant as a school shooting in another part of the country, but the sadness may affect them on a personal level either way. The silver lining is that the INFJs may find a new cause to take up – and they will pursue it wholeheartedly.

With Friends: Friends can provide the single greatest source of comfort for the INFJ, who views the world through rather less-than-rose-colored glasses. Whether they are getting worked up over the injustice of third-world orphans not having fresh drinking water or lamenting their own losses, INFJs feel the tragedy in the world and should talk it out with their friends if they are feeling particularly down about something.

Health: Not being able to affect change is one of the INFJs' biggest worries, and they tend to devote their lives (and livelihoods) to the pursuit of equality and social rights for all. Yet because they feel so passionately about righting the evils which cause so much sadness the world around, INFJs can end up misplacing guilt — onto themselves, of course — and shouldering more stress than they should on their already delicate sensibilities.

Finances: Stunned and horrified by the abuses that take place in the world or the personal tragedy that has befallen the INFJ, it can be expected that this personality type will make monetary donations to the causes that are dear to their hearts. It's less likely that INFJs will make huge, lump sum donations to one organization, and instead spread them out over a few, so it's important that they make sure they are spending within their means and don't lose track of how much they are paying out to the causes in which they so deeply believe.

14. Ease of being hurt

Positive: Being hurt easily is not the best way to go through life, but it does come with at least one unexpected plus. Early on, when faced with criticism or critique, constructive or otherwise, the INFJ learns he/she must cope or crumble. Because of this strong sense of achievement and desire to help others, while the hurt may not be forgotten or forgiven as easily as it is processed and felt, INFJs learn to move past it and move on with their lives.

Negative: But those around the INFJ probably have to learn to guard their tongues and be careful in how they act so as not to upset their emotional friend or relative. This can create some resentment, as they may think, "Why should so-and-so get preferential treatment?" For the individual him/herself, it is incredibly difficult going through life always bearing the weight of the last negative thing someone said to you – and the thing before that, and before that, and so on.

In Relationships: The easily hurt INFJs require a patient and forgiving mate, but they reciprocate these virtues tenfold. One of the best things the partner of an INFJ can do is to help this person learn to express their hurt — as opposed to bottling it up, as they are very likely to do, especially if they are in the early stages of a relationship and don't know their lover 100 percent quite yet. INFJs might feel bad, but for them, making others feel bad as well only makes them feel worse, so they have to be coaxed into letting it out. Talking about it might not work for all; instead, try writing it down in journal or letter form.

At Work: It is not generally the boss's prerogative to tiptoe around criticism, yet the high-achieving INFJ may be worth the effort, because his/her creative output is usually that person's most valuable quality in the workplace. But, it is impossible to avoid altogether, so the INFJ must simply learn to absorb the negative and use it to fuel positive action, whether it comes from the manager in charge or a coworker.

With Friends: INFJs like to joke around as much as anyone (and they usually have a lively, witty sense of humor), but sometimes the digs go a little too deep for them — that is to say, a lot of the time they can dish it out but they have a harder time taking it. Their friends should be aware that INFJs sometimes internalize things that were spoken in jest, but at the same time, those of this personality type should practice having thicker skin, especially among the people who truly love them for who they are.

Finances: INFJs are emotional and may act based on their emotions, but they tend to have the willpower to keep their money out of it. And that's a darn good thing, because if INFJs went running to the store every time someone made them feel bad, they'd be maxing out credit cards left and right. Perhaps this personality type will turn to cookies or bad TV when the going gets rough and their feelings are hurt, but their Judging aspect — with its emphasis on commitment and responsibility — keeps their bank account safe.

15. A Moody Demeanor

Positive: Trying to find out what exactly is wrong with an INFJ may feel like interrogating a tight-lipped MI6 agent who can withstand anything you throw at him/her. But at least you'll be aware that something is wrong in the first place, thanks to their penchant for moodiness. They may be able to conceal quite a bit, but they can't conceal everything, and if you're a watchful, vigilant friend, it will be fairly obvious that something is amiss and needs to be discussed.

Negative: Yet it's no fun dealing with a crab apple who won't talk about things and who has to be practically badgered into explaining what's up. It is certainly not helped that INFJs' inclination for holding things in (and down) also makes the moodiness even worse, as the situation or feeling is left unresolved thanks to their best clam impression. Sometimes you will have to just leave them alone to stew for a bit before you can make any progress.

In Relationships: The INFJ is lucky he/she has so many wonderful qualities to help balance out the moodiness. And to be fair, these types will probably try to quell the worst of it, if only to avoid having to talk about it. But, once their mates and families have learned how to handle and manage the sometimes-grumpy, sometimes-passive aggressive tendencies in their loved one, they can go back to enjoying how caring and compassionate their INFJ love bug is.

At Work: INFJs put on a happy face for everyone at work in order to mask the moodiness that lurks underneath. Their façade might slip now and then, but only to coworkers with whom they feel comfortable already. If you look closely, you might catch an eye roll; or, you can listen carefully and hear a suppressed, annoyed sigh, but INFJs would otherwise rather avoid direct grumpiness that would make them the center of the attention.

With Friends: Friends who have been there over the long haul are probably used to the INFJ's mood swings, taking it in stride. After all, when INFJs are in a good mood, there is no equal to their positive demeanor; when they are in a bad mood, well — they can be coaxed out of it by various means. Chances are, their close pals know exactly what to do or say to lighten the mood or switch gears. Crisis averted.

Health: Mood swings aren't terribly alarming in and of themselves, as we all experience sudden changes in how we feel. However, if the INFJ appears to be edging into a less controlled place, emotionally, where the mood variances become wider and more abrupt, then it could be a sign that all is not well, and professional advice should be sought. On the whole, though, INFJs should try to self-remedy their moodiness, perhaps by developing a calming mantra or practicing meditation.

Finances: Because of their strong commitment to a successful future, INFJs' money situations are less likely to be affected by their moodiness than, say, their friendships or mental health. But it never hurts for them to be aware of any spending habits that develop over time, such as sudden sadness causing impulse purchases of TV or movie sets, or happiness spurring them to call up friends for a joyful, but expensive meal. It might only feel like once in a while, but even the little purchases can knick away at their bank account.

16. Perfectionist Traits

Positive: If you need someone to do something for you – say, help you decorate before a party or look over a letter before you send it to your ex – then the INFJ is your best bet to put forth perfection. INFJs' skills and creativity shine because they seek to be the best version of themselves possible. It is admirable, inspiring, and – most importantly – a reliable trait that is always set to the "on" position, and these Feeling types are happy to reach out and help anyone who asks (more than that, they're flattered someone thought them worth asking!).

Negative: One of the most difficult tasks for the INFJ to accomplish, however, is not looking at others and expecting similar perfection in them, too. These types cannot help themselves, as they cast an eye around to their friends and family, and if they see something that doesn't match their ideals and/or standards, you will probably know about it. This is an incredibly challenging tendency for them to manage and one of their most off-putting characteristics.

In Relationships: They do want everything to be perfect, and their relationship is one of them. It starts with finding the perfect mate and then making sure to do everything right to please them. Thanks to an intuitive understanding of others, the partners of INFJs will often find that their lover lives to surprise them with the ideal gift. Children of an INFJ will know it; when they come home with a B, their straight-A parent wonders why they didn't do better.

At Work: Trust the INFJ employee to knock it out of the ballpark thanks to his/her complementary blend of ingenuity and drive. Projects won't see the light of day (or rather, a second pair of eyes) unless they are absolutely perfect, and this includes Power Points, paintings, and even first drafts of a short story or poem. If there's a downside to the INFJ's work, it's that too much perfection breeds jealousy and resentment among less gifted coworkers and peers.

With Friends: It is not uncommon for friends of INFJs to look at them with alarm when it becomes apparent that "okay" is not good enough, not where their painting for the Colors and Cocktails event is concerned. Whether it's a paint-and-wine night or what was supposed to be a fun night of Wii bowling, INFJs' propensity for perfection can sour the mood; at the same time, if they are throwing a party for their nearest and dearest, there is no question it will go off without a hitch.

Health: Perfection is a tall order, and the INFJs aim to fill it, but it can be to the detriment of their own health. The stress of matching reality to the ideals in the INFJs' Intuitive head can take its toll, because who has the time and energy to perfect every aspect of their life — their home, their work, their family, etc.? No one, but the INFJ will run him/herself ragged in the pursuit of it, missing sleep, meals, and who knows what else. INFJs need to learn to accept a little imperfection, because that's the stuff life is made of!

Finances: Like any good Judging type, INFJs keep a close eye on their bank statements. Dreamy and idealistic though they might be, these types don't mess around when it comes to their money, because they wear the mantle of responsibility and believe in setting a course now that leads to a better future. If they create a savings plan, INFJs will stick to it with laser-sharp precision, their perfectionist traits put to excellent use in this instance.

17. Loneliness

Positive: If it weren't for their loneliness, INFJs could stay in quiet seclusion for much longer than is probably healthy. Thanks to their inherent introversion, this personality type needs alone or "me" time in order to function, but they can overdo it and get too comfortable in their solitude, which is not good when there are responsibilities to be handled. Thankfully, loneliness eventually pulls them back toward other humans who need them – as family members, friends or coworkers.

Negative: Loneliness is, however, one of the characteristics that makes INFJs emotionally clingy and that can help push them toward a morose frame of mind. Sometimes, that self-imposed seclusion can be tough to dig out of, and INFJs must take care to keep their lifelines open: people to whom they can reach out and with whom they can socialize and quell that aching solace. Otherwise, they will live in a profound darkness that few of us can imagine.

In Relationships: Interestingly enough, not even loneliness will compel true INFJs to make any compromises where their partners are concerned (as is evinced by their idealization of the perfect partner — later on in this book). However, after INFJs withdraw into themselves for a period of solitude to recharge their batteries, it is often to their romantic mates that they reach out first when they need human-to-human contact once again, since they choose partners with whom they feel a deep bond that can withstand even the most introverted of episodes.

At Work: Loneliness at work may occur for the INFJ because he/she sought a career that was based on independence to begin with. Disliking crowds, combined with their stubborn nature often makes INFJs the perfect candidates for solitary work environments. But no man is an island forever. Still, one taste of group work will probably send these personality types happily back to their quiet corner, and loneliness is soon forgotten.

With Friends: INFJs might not always feel like reaching out to friends, even when they are feeling the grip of loneliness. What started out as a voluntary hiatus from company could turn into a situation where they begin to get trapped inside their own heads, thinking that no one has texted them yet because no one has even noticed they were gone. Not so, INFJ, but friends of this type could help alleviate the situation by sending an email or something to check in, just in case.

Health: Loneliness in and of itself isn't a major health issue, but if it becomes a pervasive factor in the INFJ's life, if he/she goes weeks without interacting with anyone and can't seem to muster the effort through his/her loneliness to do so, then it could be time to seek professional advice. Introverts can be difficult to get a read on because they can be so distant, but they usually have at least a few people close enough to them to notice when something is amiss.

Finances: INFJs' finances should not suffer too much as a direct result of their loneliness, unless they are spending money on pizza and pay-per-view movies that they don't have. In some ways, their finances can be bolstered by the alone time, since they aren't out throwing down $40 for a single meal with friends or going shopping at the mall. And some INFJs might end up using their loneliness to create their master work, a piece that will bring in income.

18. Idealization of a perfect relationship

Positive: Seeking the very best people to complement you as you journey through life is both metaphorically uplifting and an arduous task that requires patience and a heart that is ever-seeking. Relationships come in all forms, not just romantic, and INFJs' desire to match each and every one with a predetermined ideal is just part of their ongoing process of self-improvement. Good relationships, after all, help us to be better people.

Negative: Of course, the downside is that perfection is an elusive quality that can, more often than not, be a figment of the imagination and nothing more. Sometimes, INFJs can be misguided by their quest for what, in their minds, is the ideal relationship, whether it's a friendship or how they get on with their mothers and fathers. It can be difficult for this personality type, therefore, to accept people and situations for what they really are.

In Relationships: Don't be surprised if you meet INFJs who are older, unmarried, and yet still seeking that fantasy partner. Either no one ever told them that it is unlikely that someone is going to match every little bullet on their list, or someone did, and they rejected the idea outright because they know – and there's that stubborn trait – they just know the right person is out there. They'd rather be single and alone than paired up with someone who isn't a perfect mate.

At Work: Finding the right work relationships is tough because the INFJ isn't the kind of person who easily opens up and makes a lot of friends. To make matters more difficult, INFJs want to work among (and for) people whom they feel share their values. This is yet another example of why this introverted personality tends to seek more independent employment opportunities, but if the right environment can be found, then the INFJ will have outstanding work output.

With Friends: Friends hold your hand when you need comfort, but they are also there to kick you in the butt when you are being ridiculous. INFJs aren't often ridiculous, but when it comes to their search for the "perfect" mate, they might require a little butt kickin'. If their friends can't tell them to stop dumping people for not living up to their lofty standards, who will? No one. This is why it's important for INFJs to at least take into consideration their friends' admonishments that a weird big toe isn't cause for breakup.

Health: When we are in a good relationship with someone, we are happy. It's not that you can't be happy when you're single, but humans are social animals who, at their basest level, appreciate the benefits of being paired up with someone. INFJs might be perfectly content in their single state, but they are doomed to unhappiness if their singleness is a result of failed relationships that end because the INFJs refuse to settle for anything less than perceived perfection. In the long run, that can have surprisingly adverse effects on their health.

Finances: Like many Feeling types, the INFJ probably doesn't have "millionaire" on the list of traits that describe an ideal partner, feeling as they do that it's what inside that matters. But this Judging type also isn't going to settle for someone who has been in the process of looking for a new job — for the past five years. So while the INFJ might have rather lofty standards in general, at least they are wise enough to want someone whose financial ambitions match theirs.

19. Fear of Rejection

Positive: Fears might hold you back, but they also keep you safe. INFJs feel nothing lightly, and if they fear something in particular, then there is a good chance it is their strong, in-tune intuition ringing alarm bells and telling them to avoid something at all costs. These personality types learn early on to trust their gut, and while others might look at them and wonder why they hold back, INFJs knows that if they fear rejection, it is likely for good reason.

Negative: Yet life is full of unknown quantities, and that is perhaps the major flaw in the INFJs' super self-trust. Instinct or experience may have taught them that "going for it" in a given situation will likely result in their rejection, but life is utterly unpredictable at times, and people or moments can surprise us all with their reactions or outcomes. So, sometimes being held back by that fear of rejection can result in some pretty unfortunate missed opportunities, like a dream job that only seemed out of reach.

In Relationships: Once they are secure in a happy relationship, INFJs are supremely pleasing mates on many levels. Yet finding that partner can be a challenge when these types think they know that the beautiful blonde on the subway or the gorgeous man in glasses from book club will say no if they put themselves out there and ask that person to go get a cup of coffee. This fear also informs their behavior in a relationship to the extent that they worry a misstep will result in a breakup and a broken heart.

At Work: INFJs dream big and work hard, yet still grapple with the nagging suspicion in the backs of their minds that the huge promotion will pass them over. Artistic INFJs may agonize over putting their creative babies out there for the entire world to judge; imagine INFJ Jerry Seinfeld pitching his idea for a "show about nothing" — what were the chances such an inconspicuous plotline would go on to form one of the most influential TV programs ever created?

With Friends: "Go on, ask her out!" a friend will urge, nudging his INFJ buddy in the ribs. "Naw..." the INFJ will respond, even though the pretty woman on the other end of the bar has been looking in his direction and smiling all night. And what does it take for the INFJ to overcome his fear of rejection? That's right — his pal, going over to the woman himself and giving her the INTJ's number. That's what friends are for!

Health: With any luck, the INFJ's fear of rejection won't have much impact on his/her health, confining itself mainly to his/her social life. But rejection comes in all shapes and forms, including professional rejection in which the INFJ might feel under-qualified for a promising position that comes with excellent benefits — like health benefits, of which the INFJ might be sorely in need. The INFJ definitely won't be getting those new glasses any time soon if he/she doesn't even send in a resume and cover letter to apply.

Finances: When the INFJ is finally ready to buy a house, you can bet he/she is going to be a nervous wreck before he/she goes into the bank to formally discuss a mortgage. But, if anything, INTJs' fear that the bank will laugh at them outright causes them to over-prepare, starting from the time they began to sock away money for a down payment, up to the very day of the meeting, when the paperwork they must bring in gets clammy from hand sweat.

20. Dislike of Noise

Positive: Thanks to their intense dislike for noise, the environment in which you can find INFJs is serene — the perfect place for a deep, one-on-one chat if you have been invited into their inner sanctum. Because they like to shut out the raucous cacophony of the outside world, the INFJ has likely created a home and/or work space which lets them breathe deep, focus, and work on both themselves and their personal goals, both of which aim to better the world.

Negative: This particular dislike, however, means that if you want to get the INFJ to accompany you to a rock concert, well...you have your work cut out for you. It can also be a bit bizarre if you're in public with him/her, come upon a noisy crowd, and you turn and find that your INFJ friend has completely shut down as a result. Yes, it is a little bit embarrassing, and it's equally unpleasant for those of this personality type to constantly have to explain themselves.

In Relationships: Dislike of noise shouldn't bear too much on their romantic relationships (unless, of course, they have found marital bliss with a drummer), but it can affect how they interact with their children. Children, as you may know, often come with two volumes: loud and screeching, and there is no telling which yours will favor until you try to take them to church. This might make the perfectionist INFJs cringe down to their toes, but they're luckily gifted with much understanding and caring as a parent.

At Work: INFJs may have a propensity for the written word, but unless they have been passionately moved by a cause, they will avoid noisy professions like journalism for more staid writing — the type that can be accomplished with a lap top, in a quiet café or home office. Whatever their workspace, it will reflect their innate need for calm, so expect to find headphones or even a sound machine nearby so that they may drown out chatter with Ocean Sounds #5.

With Friends: There's really no dragging the INFJ out to the club, unless you want the person you're dancing with to yell over the music, "Who's that girl with her hands over her ears?" INFJs just are not having any of it, and while that can be a bummer for their friends who love a wild night on the town and fuzzy hearing the next day, it is better for everyone if the INFJ just stays in and catches up with everyone the next day.

Health: Even if it makes the youngest INFJ out there seem like a crotchety old man, this personality type's dislike of noise is a plus when it comes to health. For one thing, it keeps INFJS away from activities that could have a damaging effect on their long-term hearing. For another, it ensures that INFJs seeks out calm and relaxation, something fewer adults make an effort to do today more than ever.

Finances: If the INFJ isn't hitting the clubs every weekend or heading to concerts or music festivals (or really, anywhere else there's a crowd), at least they aren't spending money recklessly or impulsively. As much of a downer as that can seem to be to the people who want their company, building their finances for the future is important to INFJs, who likely don't mind missing out on expensive, loud activities.

21. Easily Distracted

Positive: If there is one positive when it comes to the easily distracted, it's that this personality type is simply curious and interested, especially in topics that relate to the human experience, like tragedy or suffering, which they will want to rush into and help abate at once. There are so many people out there who need the succor of others, and the INFJ wants to be in many places, all at once, offering it to them. The scope of INFJs' caring is admirable; these are people who will actually do something to help those around them.

Negative: The downside is that, while INFJs are often imbued with a strong sense of duty and honor that propels them into action, one cause may suffer because they have taken up with another before completing the first task (or they might find themselves called away from their families by work). What they need is someone or something to help center them and keep them focused, so that this easy distraction does not inhibit their ability to help so many.

In Relationships: INFJs may be distracted by another person when they are in a serious relationships, but it likely won't be an extra lover. Picture a painter inflamed with the lovely subject of his/her latest work, or the social worker who seemingly forgets he/she has a family at home when putting in late hours to help a client. Luckily, the families of INFJs know that they have an almost inhuman love for their loved ones; "out of sight, out of mind" need not apply.

At Work: It is unfortunate that INFJs have a tendency to let their minds wander, but the fact is, no matter what field they

56

are working in, if the job they have to do is compelling enough, they will be able to stay on task. However, if it is menial work that does not challenge and inspire them, then expect distraction to come in the form of daydreaming about a career in which they are moving and shaking the world — as this personality type is so apt to do.

With Friends: Friends are probably used to the INFJ saying they'd be there at the coffee shop at a certain time and then showing up 15 minutes late because they "got distracted" by something. INFJs do hate being late, however, and will strive to make it up to their pals as best as they can, so the trade between 15 minutes of waiting alone and a free coffee isn't such a bad deal, all things considered.

Health: INFJs tend to be pretty on point when it comes to their health, but they take a lot onto their plates and can end up forgetful. On the plus side, however, if the INFJ is suffering from some sort of illness, he/she is easily distracted and can be moved to think about something else. The next time you go to visit your INFJ friend in the hospital, bring him/her a good book, a tough puzzle, or just a lot of fun gossip, and you'll qualify for a nurse in his/her eyes.

Finances: While INFJs can get distracted, their Judging aspect ensures that these otherwise focused and detail-oriented individuals come right back to whatever they were examining. Perhaps their check books will go unbalanced for a few days, but the INFJ has it on the to-do list and will make sure that it's finished — as well as getting all the bills paid — with the methodical air of one who knows what his/her business is about.

22. Moved to Tears by Books or Movies

Positive: Big Hollywood producers could ask for no more perfect an audience than the INFJ, who not only cries when sad/joyful things happen, but also belly laughs during the comical parts and hides behind his/her fingers during the scary bits. Authors, too, might as well write the INFJ a check, because if a novel has moved someone of this type to an actual, physical response, then you can bet this personality type is recommending the read to his/her friends.

Negative: What was that last line before the screen faded to black? No one in the theater knows because your INFJ friend was bawling hysterically like a heartbroken Jane Austen heroine. You might want to read the reviews before going out or taking out the INFJ to the theater, because he/she will likely embarrass the heck out of you, and next time you want to see something together, wait until it's on Netflix.

In Relationships: For the person in love with an INFJ, seeing him/her sob over a movie or a book might just be the cutest/sweetest thing ever (again, provided you are on your own couch in your own living room). What's more, crying has a way of purifying the soul (and the body) — notice how good you feel after a hard cry, as if all your sense are awake? Cry on, you emotional INFJ, cry like no one except your partner is watching.

At Work: Well, there is no hiding when the INFJ is reading on his or her lunch break, because you will look over and see the tears falling. This characteristic can also have another unforeseen consequence: if the book or movie depicts a worthy cause, the INFJ may adopt it as his/her own and be moved to use the resources at his/her disposal – some professional – to help those less fortunate.

With Friends: Even if your reaction isn't quite as dramatic as you imagine your INFJ friend's was, you can always count on them for a good book or movie suggestion, particularly if you want something heartfelt. Plus, there is something totally endearing about having that one buddy who cannot hold his/her tears in when it comes to reading and viewing material — and you always have the reassurance of knowing if you were at the theater with a tear rolling down your cheek, you weren't the only one.

Health: Crying is healthy for numerous reasons, and because the INFJ prefers to spend his/her leisure time reading or watching movies or TV, there's a good chance these types are sniffling on the regular — and reaping the health benefits. Far from being a cold fish or some kind of sociopath, INFJs' blubbery ways are a good measure of their strong sense of empathy and overall well-being as an emotional person.

Finances: Because crying feels so good, it's like a little high for INFJs, and while they probably won't go broke buying books and movies to fuel their addiction, they should watch their spending and make sure they are staying within their means (and leaving enough cash in the bank account to pay the bills). As long as the INFJs use their "funny money" (cash for fun things) and stay away from the bills allotted to necessities, there are much worse things on which they could be spending their hard-earned dollars!

23. High Sensitivity to the Moods of Others

Positive: If you are one of those people who says "nothing" when someone asks what's wrong, but there is very clearly something wrong that need to talk about, then you want an INFJ as a friend, because he or she knows something is up. And, even better, he/she will know whether you are the kind of person who needs to be coaxed into conversation (at which point the floodgates open and your woes spill out) or left alone until you broach the subject. INFJs are just that good, but they honestly don't look at it as a talent or skill — it's simply who they are.

Negative: On the downside, though, being sensitive to others' moods can also alter INFJs' moods, so even that crab in line at Starbucks who takes his/her misery out on the cashier can have an overwhelmingly negative effect on these types as they stand in line and witness someone else's unjust cruelty. It is a difficult way to go through life, always absorbing the energy of others.

In Relationships: It is nice to have a partner who cares so much about you and will tiptoe around your feelings so that you are never hurt, but the partners of INFJs must also be careful about how much of their negative mood they put out there, because their mate will just soak it right up like a sponge. On the other hand, consider your happiness and your joy infectious; you will find no more of an enthusiastic cheerleader than the INFJ mate.

At Work: It might be difficult for the INFJ to face Mondays at work because all the morose faces will likely take their toll. It can also be difficult for the always interpreting, always analytical INFJ to stop reading into the comments of others; any old email might read particularly snippy and throw the INFJ into a tailspin of worry that he/she is the cause of that irritation, when in reality the coworker who sent it is just upset because of an argument at home.

With Friends: Introverts absorb the energy of the people around them, thus making social interaction rather overwhelming (to say nothing of draining), but the INFJs' added Feeling aspect — which allows them to easily empathize with others — creates a kind of perfect storm, where the INFJ is deeply and especially sensitive to their closest friends' moods. Their buddy's bad day can easily become their bad day, yet because they are so willing to stick around and help their friends feel better, the prolonged exposure can take its toll.

Health: The life of an INFJ can be exhausting physically, but it is the emotional toll that this personality type has to watch out for. Constantly absorbing and feeling affected by the moods of others is a difficult and sometimes frustrating way to go through life, because while it is delightful to feel the joy of others, it can be draining to likewise experience their sorrows, their anger, and their unhappiness. INFJs should make a concentrated effort not to let others' moods touch them at their core.

Finances: Thankfully, INFJs aren't likely to let the influence of others' moods affect how they spend, so even if their sibling is down on his/her luck and in need of a loan, this personality type isn't going to give it up without an iron-clad agreement of repayment. INFJs' Judging aspect saves the day yet again, and while they like to think the best of people whenever possible, they are also firmly committed to their own financial health and future.

24. Easily Overwhelmed

Positive: Being easily overwhelmed isn't all bad; especially not for the introspective INFJ, who knows when to withdraw and retreat to find inner peace and calm. While they may show their frustration with tears in private, at least INFJs have the good sense to be honest themselves, and are always able to identify how they are feeling and what they can do to remedy bad moods. INFJs like to enjoy a variety of activities interspersed with their (hopefully fulfilling) work, and those feelings of being overwhelmed are most satisfying when they are methodically being vanquished.

Negative: Yet that feeling of being overwhelmed is still difficult for INFJs, because these personality types are so used to achieving and raising the bar. It can be very jarring for others to see these introverted individuals withdraw so completely when the going gets tough, and they may view them, incorrectly, as weak. They aren't, but they have to do what needs to be done in order to bounce back and get back in the saddle.

In Relationships: Because the INFJs are always trying to be the perfect mates, it is not uncommon for them to get overwhelmed in a relationship, no matter if they have been dating for two months or 20 years. It takes patient partners with steady, gentle hands to calm their stressed-out beloved, but the emotional rewards for the one who can stick by the INFJ's side are myriad and lasting.

At Work: Trust that even if the INFJ gets overwhelmed before anyone else at the workplace, he/she knows what is needed in order to get back on track. Or if they don't know right away, you can trust that INFJs' innate creativity will come up with something on the fly. They are reliable and dependable, and their care for their work is so abiding that they can overcome a mountain of unfinished paperwork.

With Friends: INFJs, like most Introverts, like to keep a tight circle of friends. It's not just that they prefer quality friendships over acquaintances (in which you don't know if the other person would come through for you if you were to have a flat on the side of the highway), but also that when INFJs are faced with a large group of people, they tend to react to being overwhelmed by shutting down completely. Sure, INFJs have to put their big-kid pants on now and then when it comes to crowds, but they are at their best in a group if they know each person personally.

Health: INFJs have big hearts, and it's not uncommon for them to take on a full-time career, a family, charitable activities, school-related activities, and even favors for friends. That's a heck of a lot of obligations, and while INFJs rarely resent the fact, it can be damaging to their health if they never have any downtime or "me" time. It's important for everyone to get away once in a while, so the INFJ should take care to use up those vacation days and pencil in some fun, like a spa day for the ladies or a guys' night out for the men.

Finances: It's not likely that INFJs will forget to pay a bill (they have life's minutia down pat!) because they were overwhelmed with everything going on in their lives, but the enormity of life's expenses can get to them once in a while. Between rent or mortgage, bills, family expenses, gas, etc. — who doesn't get a little beat down once in a while? But INFJs simply need to remember that they are good at saving, and as long as they follow their own intuition when it comes to money matters, they should be just fine.

25. Sensitive Skin

Positive: Along with a profound understanding of what makes up people's inner emotions, the INFJ often finds that his/her skin is highly sensitive, enabling this type to feel and understand the physical as well. It also makes for a more richly lived life, one that draws joy out of a full-body experience in a place like an exotic market, where the textures of fabrics and seeds intoxicate, please, awaken, and linger.

Negative: But then heat and cold and other unpleasant physical feelings are felt that much more acutely. The INFJ may be the first one to complain when the snow falls and the first to badmouth an exceedingly hot day in spring, as well. If an INFJ burns his/her hand on a hot pan, expect to hear the yelp of pain a good three towns over. And INFJs may suffer from that ghastly green skin which occurs when there's cheap jewelry on one's hand.

In Relationships: Let's keep things PG here, but sensitive skin makes for a very positive physical experience, if you get what we're saying. That, coupled with the INFJ's ability to get a very accurate reading on other people, means that in relationships when the heat is on, it is on. Typical INFJs love to please and be pleased in equal measures, and their generous nature means that whatever they feel when they are touched, they want to reciprocate.

At Work: Never one to crave sociability (even if their friendliness and kindness makes them quite popular), don't be surprised if INFJs in the workplace shrink away from much contact with their coworkers — even from a friendly hug on a their birthday or a clap on the back for a job well done. And they might also be the ones who bring a bulky sweater in the summer because the air conditioning is just too darn intense right over their desk.

With Friends: INFJs usually look at their friends with envy when it comes to all matters involving the skin. Whether it's their friend's perfect bronze glow (versus their own lobsteresque color after a day at the beach), or the fact that others can buy cheapie jewelry and wear it without a problem while the INFJ's skin turns an alarming shade of puke green, INFJs learn through the years, by comparison with their buddies, that their skin needs special care and attention.

Health: INFJs, like their INFP cousins, tend toward skin that requires a little something extra in terms of nourishment. This can mean special potions and lotions, extra SPF sunblock, and even makeup that has been carefully crafted and is free of chemicals. It can take a lot of work to maintain the INFJ complexion, but it's worth the effort, because a healthful INFJ is a glowing INFJ, and these types have a way of making themselves look like they were born glowing and as dewy as the petal of a rose.

Finances: Sensitive skin can take a surprising chunk of cash to maintain, because products that offer the benefits INFJs require are always more expensive (and in some cases, might have to be purchased online, with the additional expense of shipping). Smart INFJs, however, could turn to DIY solutions, as there is an abundance of basic household products (like sugar and olive oil, for instance) that can be turned into inexpensive, yet effective substitutions for the stuff you buy at the store.

26. Enjoys Complexity

Positive: Never one to shy from a challenge, the INFJ relishes layer upon layer of new information about a subject or person. When the going gets tough, INFJs stick around to solve whatever puzzle has everyone else stumped, and they will usually do so in such a creative and imaginative way that they emerge the hero of the day. Complexity gives life its richness in the INFJ view, and these types can appreciate it as no other personality type.

Negative: Their enjoyment of the complex, however, can lead to the INFJ trying to delve deeper into the meaning of something, even when the facts are simple and straightforward. This can lead to a tailspin of self-doubt when INFJs' seeking comes up empty-handed. One of the great weaknesses in INFJs' personality is failing to comprehend the big picture because they get so lost in the minute details, like a writer who cannot stop playing around with a single sentence in an essay of 20 pages.

In Relationships: The INFJ is a complex individual him/herself, the kind of person who has layers upon layers that could take years to pull back, and even then, his/her most beloved life partner would never learn all of his/her secrets and mysteries. It makes sense, then, that this onion-like personality type seeks the same in mates, an equal about whom the INFJ can enjoy a lifetime of learning new things.

At Work: INFJs may be gifted writers and artists, not just mediocre hobbyists, because their enjoyment of the complex allows them to imbue their work with deeper meanings and symbolism, the kind of thing readers or viewers have to work for in order to fully enjoy the creation. This also translates well in the sciences, in which math, biology, chemistry, and physics all convene in puzzles that, if unraveled, help solve the mysteries of the universe. If INFJs can combine their need for income with their genuine love for the complexities of life and/or art, their happiness is almost palpable.

With Friends: INFJs would never turn away a potential friend who is seemingly "too complex" for most people to get to know. In fact, that kind of layered personality is extremely interesting to the INFJ who is him/herself a multifaceted individual with much more to them than is on the surface. And while someone might seem complex, the Intuitive INFJ is capable of penetrating deep down to the person's basic core, where basic truths, principles, and values lie.

Health: The INFJ might not have any formal medical training, but he/she wants to see his/her hospital chart all the same. In fact, the next time the INFJ stays at a hospital, it shouldn't come as a surprise to anyone if he/she spends his/her waking moments learning as much about the real-life running of the place as he/she can, simply because the complexities of one's daily life as a doctor or nurse in a bustling medical facility are downright fascinating to the inquisitive and intelligent INFJ.

Finances: INFJs might not be born CPAs, but they are hands-on when it comes to their finances, and they wouldn't mind learning a little bit of what their accountant knows, as well as the basics of tax law. Knowledge is power, and INFJs are often formidably intellectual, taking pleasure in absorbing new information — particularly information that is challenging and causes them to stretch their intellects in order to achieve some form of mastery. While a career in accounting is probably not in their wheelhouse, understanding the complexities of financial management is.

27. Likes to Analyze Patterns

Positive: The world around us is set out in patterns that, if comprehended, give the lucky discoverers a deeper understanding of how and why things work. INFJs have a natural ability and affinity for such thinking, and their quickness to "get it" – whether it's numbers, human behavior or images – is part of what helps them work out the tough problems that elude others. If you ever took the GRE and recall the verbal portion that featured those dreaded analogies — the INFJ probably rocked those without breaking a sweat.

Negative: But again, like their taste for the complex, INFJs' affinity for analyzing patterns can have the undesirable effect of getting them lost in their own heads and thoughts, so focused on the small things that the most obvious details fly right over them. Patterns, of course, only make up a small portion of a whole; so, INFJs must actively take a step back and place their limited view in the context of the greater situation.

In Relationships: We are never so predictable in life as we are in our relationships, as serial daters will again and again make the same mistakes that prohibit emotional growth and progress. If nothing else, INFJs' flair for pattern analysis can be used to strengthen their relationships by allowing them to find the source of conflict – which is usually the same (i.e. "We have this argument over and over again!") – and then helping them actively resolve it.

At Work: Throw the INFJ into a scientific lab and you might find this person as happy as a clam, working independently and at his/her own pace, chitchat at a minimum. The sciences are all about patterns, so this is a field in which the INFJ could particularly shine, especially in the theoretical subfields, where patterns might be best explained and analyzed with the application of creativity and original thinking. INFJs' pattern analysis is also helpful by way of managing other people, much like it is in their personal relationships, because finding the root cause of ongoing workplace conflict makes solving the issue that much easier.

With Friends: INFJs might not have the down-to-earth approach to life that Sensing types do, but they are still excellent at dispensing advice to friends thanks to their own outside vantage point and ability to step back, look at the their friends' behaviors through a wide lens, and then make sense of all the chaos. It is easy for the INFJ to pick out a pattern of behavior — say, one that has had a negative influence on their friend's dating life and relationships? And you can count on the Feeling INFJs to find the most tactful way to address the issue and try to help their friends evolve.

Health: Thanks to their Intuitive aspect, once INFJs sit down and allows themselves the chance to think about their health, they can easily deduce whether or not certain symptoms have been occurring regularly. That can make it a lot easier for them to get a reasonable diagnosis for less serious ailments using the Internet, and it also helps their doctor to diagnose whatever is wrong if the illness appears to be more serious.

Finances: The ability to analyze patterns is a great strength for INFJs when it comes to their financial management, because getting into the rhythm of one's monthly cash flow ensures that bills are paid on time. INFJs can also take an objective look at their spending and see if they need to cut back — perhaps they notice that whenever they go to the movies, a trip to their favorite organic foods store always follows, since it's conveniently right across the street.

28. Likes to Analyze Motivations of Others

Positive: One thing is for sure: no one is getting one over the INJF. If you were thinking about trying to pull the wool over this personality's eyes, then you have another thing coming your way; he or she will be pondering your every move and comment, and will likely come out on top. It's a good thing, too, because a person as caring, compassionate, and kind as the INFJ could easily be taken advantage of by less benevolent individuals.

Negative: Still, if you were trying to plan a surprise birthday party for the INFJ in your life, you might want to reconsider because he/she cannot help but put two and two together. This penchant for analyzing the motives of others can also contribute to the INFJs' more stand-offish qualities; they are well known for being notoriously difficult to get to know, because they are taking a step back and trying to figure out why you want to befriend them. Not the most endearing quality, especially for more Extraverted people who are used to absorbing new friends into their stratosphere with ease.

In Relationships: This goes double for those who seek to date the INFJ, because romantic relationships involve so much more opening of the self than does just being friends or acquaintances. Partners who can withstand the suspicious nature of the INFJ is a worthy mate, indeed, particularly if they can put up with that look INFJs get on their faces as they are puzzling out what you meant by that huffy use of the word "again." And children of the INFJ might as well learn early that there will be no sneaking behind their parents' backs; their mother or father will see right through every little lie.

At Work: It is noted that INJFs may not be whizzes when it comes to technical workplace software, but they are apt managers of people. Part of solving the riddle for why people do the same things over and over is finding the basic motivating factor that pops up again and again, compelling them to act the way they do. In this task, INFJs are reliable and acute, and while they might prefer independent work conditions, they are assets to large groups of people.

With Friends: INFJs aren't suspicious sorts at heart, but they do like to take a step back and look at the big picture when it comes to their friends. Usually this comes in the form of reminiscing over good times and thinking about what an amazing journey they have had with someone, but it can also come in handy if someone is taking advantage of the INFJ's generous Feeling output. If the INFJ can deduce that someone is clearly using him/her in a way that they don't like, he/she can kick that jerk to the curb and get on with his/her life.

Health: Nothing is more alarming to INFJs than a doctor or nurse who is doing something to them and not telling them why. A blood test when they were supposed to be there for a routine physical, or a deeply wrinkled frown accompanied by an uncomfortable throat clearing is reason enough for INFJs to wonder what the heck is going on and how many months do they have left? Should they update their will? Where their health is concerned (and their healthcare professionals), INFJs need to pay more attention to what is being said than what isn't.

Finances: If someone hits up an INFJ for a cash loan, this personality type might not be the sort to ask directly, "What for?" (preferring, as they do, to be models of tact), but you can bet the INFJ will spend the next week musing over it. In truth, INFJs have a right to know where the money they are lending out is being spent, so they shouldn't shy away from asking directly. They might enjoy pondering their sister's sudden need for $500, but it makes better sense to just find out that it's to get her boyfriend's name tattooed on her lip.

29. Doesn't Like Too Much Attention

Positive: Quick — who is the most annoying, attention-seeking person on your Facebook feed? Whoever it is, that person is not an INFJ, because these personality types don't like to create a scene. A little recognition now and then for a job well done is right up INFJs' alley, and this mild approach to attention is part of what makes them such decent people to be around. You will never have to worry about your INFJ friend showboating at an inappropriate moment — or any moment, really.

Negative: It's hard to imagine a bride who doesn't want all the attention on her wedding day, yet the INFJ is just that sort; in fact, bride or groom, when it comes to such events, INFJs would probably rather skip it entirely to avoid having hundreds of pairs of eyes on them for hours. This can make INFJs a bit of a party pooper in situations in which they are supposed to soak up all the attention, like birthday parties or baby showers, especially if the family's expectation is that major life events are to be celebrated loud and proud.

In Relationships: Always thinking about his or her partner: that's INFJs in a relationship, and it is part of what makes these types such wonderful people with whom to share a life. If they were a houseplant, they'd be a desert rose: a brilliant addition to any household, yet surprisingly low-maintenance when it comes to daily tending. They're not completely averse to receiving attention, but their partners will likely never feel taxed by the effort.

At Work: At stated earlier, there is a definite distinction between needing attention and simply wanting recognition for the work that has been done, and the INFJ knows this difference well. He or she does not require a ticker tape parade every time they do something correctly, but whenever they do something that's over and above what was asked, a little praise will go a long way toward boosting their self-esteem and making them feel as if they contributed.

With Friends: To the casual observer, INFJs among their closest friends might look like Extraverts because they are having a great time, laughing and telling jokes, perhaps even commanding all the attention from the group once in a while. What they don't know is that INFJs are notorious wallflowers who only get like this when they are with the people they know and trust the very most, and that outside of these conditions, the INFJ would rather sink into a hole in the ground than have everyone looking at them.

Health: As the Scots say, "Dinna fash yourself," which roughly translates to "Don't make a fuss," and that could be the INFJ's motto. When INFJs are sick or injured, they are the ones who are less likely to go see a doctor, so it's really up to those around them to put their foot down and say, "You are going. Like it or not." Then, when they have been diagnosed, INFJs need to let other people help them out, make their soup, fetch things from their car, etc. Sometimes, INFJs need to have a little bit of a fuss made over them, and they can always repay the kindness in some thoughtful way.

Finances: INFJs are a modest type, and while they aren't the sorts to boast about any old accomplishment, they are positively closed up when it comes to their finances. The wealthy INFJ is not going to buy a flashy car or wear head-to-toe labels, because drawing attention to "money status" is positively crass in INFJs' eyes. Think of them as a kind of anti-Donald Trump — happy to use their well-earned wealth on themselves and others in a generous way, but in no fashion looking for acknowledgment.

30. Cautious

Positive: In today's world, danger lurks in so many places – many of them completely inconspicuous – that the chances of being harmed, or having the ones you love harmed, are greater than ever. Thankfully, INFJs have a kind of super sensor built into them, an uber-intuition that is, more often than not, right on the nose when it comes to danger. They are not overly cautious, but when they preach it or anticipate it, the warning comes with good reason.

Negative: Although their intuition is strong and steady, it is possible for INFJs to miss their mark, and they may caution themselves or others against something that turns out harmless. This translates to missed opportunities, and whether it's that once-in-a-lifetime chance to cliff dive in Europe or a job that seemed too good to be true, sometimes erring on the side of caution means sitting out unnecessarily and watching others wistfully.

In Relationships: Their henpecking mothers might complain about how they'll never have grandchildren at this rate, but the cautious INFJs know that slow and steady wins the race — or in this case, the long-lasting, mutually fulfilling relationship. For this personality type it is all about quality over quantity, and INFJs' natural caution is at its most present when seeking mates with whom share their lives. Because, after all, the INFJ doesn't let just anyone get under the surface.

At Work: Because INFJs loathe confrontation and conflict, they will likely interact with great caution in their work setting when there are coworkers. This means being careful not to step on any toes, but also exercising extreme stinginess when it comes to discussing their personal lives. As a result, this might lead to some isolation in workplaces in which employees are expected to function more as a team (like an office or retail setting).

With Friends: Someone has to be kind of a stick in the mud, and it might as well be the INFJ, who admonished his/her friends from a young age that jumping off that high, abandoned bridge into the creek below just looked like a very bad idea. And what should occur but the following month? Someone tried it and ended up in a coma! These tendencies will follow INFJs into adulthood, and though their friends might roll their eyes, INFJs could really be saving them from harm.

Health: INFJs plan to stick around on this earth for as long as possible, so you can bet these cautious sorts have been taking preventative measures where their health is concerned. Vitamins, exercise, advanced screenings — whatever it is that could help keep their hearts ticking in the long run is a good step as far as INFJs are concerned, and they find that saying, "An ounce of prevention is worth a pound of cure," to have been written specifically for them.

Finances: Without a doubt, INFJs are sensible when it comes to their money. They like to find a bargain, they like to compare prices, and they want real input when it comes to making big purchase decisions. INFJs are not, for instance, going to fall for a pyramid scheme, and they will, when the time comes, look at a dozen houses before choosing the one on which they make an offer. This cautious spending allows them to build up savings, something many adults neglect to do, and it keeps their credit score high, so that they're attractive lending prospects at the bank.

31. Easily Frightened

Positive: Don't expect the INFJ to go wandering down into the basement at night, even when those thumping noises persist for hours. These types have seen enough horror movies – all right, they have at least heard of enough horror movies – to know that nothing good happens when the person all alone in the house goes downstairs. In all seriousness, their penchant for being frightened more easily than others is yet another example of their involuntary self-preservation.

Negative: Those aforementioned horror flicks? Yeah, don't bother trying to get your INFJ friend to hit the movie theater with you for a ghoulish double feature. INFJs can be a bit of a wet blanket when it comes to situations that seem like they might devolve – even remotely – into something terrifying. So, you'll have to find someone else for those haunted houses, free fall amusement park rides, and dark cave explorations. Further, it can be difficult to take someone seriously when you hear them shrieking like a banshee over a tiny little centipede that is crawling along the wall.

In Relationships: Is there anything scarier than falling in love? Once an INFJ falls, he/she falls hard, but that doesn't make the baring his/her soul any easier. In fact, it makes it that much more difficult, because INFJs who have been bitten by the love bug are open nerves, emotionally vulnerable despite their best efforts to keep themselves safe from harm. That is a terrifying prospect for anyone, but the Feeling INFJs know how painful it can be to have one's heart broken — and they know how easily a relationship can come crashing down around them.

At Work: Type A-personality bosses are frightening enough for regular folks, but the INFJ – who is ultrasensitive to criticism to begin with, and who slides away from confrontation with the ease of a timid eel – may want to consider a different job. A worrier by nature, the INFJ will probably suffer under a boss who is less-than-tactful, because fear of losing his/her job and/or fear that the work being produced isn't good enough will always be a debilitating issue.

With Friends: That screaming from the other room? That was just your INFJ friend reacting to the sight of a little spider crawling across the floor. In instances like that, it's hard not to laugh, but say the group wants to go zip-lining or ride an awesome new rollercoaster, and the INFJ is the only one who refuses to go out of fear for his/her safety. It's no fun having a scaredy-cat around, so those of this personality type could and should make an effort where friends are concerned, and try to conquer some of their more irrational fears. Who knows, they might end up enjoying the things that frightened them!

Health: While panic over a weird lump is not helpful, at least INFJs are willing to pick up the phone and make an appointment with their doctor (which is more than can be said for some other types). In the meantime, the INFJ should try to calm his/her active imagination, think about something else and quit obsessing about what it *could* be. Fear over the unknown, in this instance, could actually lay a great deal of stress on INFJs' bodies and make them feel even worse.

Finances: Not that INFJs would ever default on a loan or not have enough to pay their credit card bill, but if the collection agency were to make a call to this personality type, they'd have found their most receptive (and terrified) audience. What is more likely when it comes to INFJs' easy fear and their finances is that these types' unwillingness to make any big mistakes where their money is concerned can turn them into Scrooges, so afraid of spending their money in an irresponsible way that they cling to every penny.

32. **Intelligent**

Positive: Intelligence comes in many forms, and the INFJ is well-informed through reading, experience, and intuition. INFJs can and do use their ample talents consistently for good, focusing all that brain power toward changing the world and making it a better place to be. While they are not known to be the most scholarly personality, others seek out INFJs for their wisdom and their guidance, particularly when it comes to handling other people, a topic about which the INFJ is especially intelligent.

Negative: All that intelligence, however, can make for one very stubborn personality. Armed with their facts and observations, INFJs will take a stance and refuse to budge from it, making them some of the most maddeningly bullish people you will ever meet. To make matters worse, they are usually right, because hey, they are smart people who cover their bases; however, that doesn't make them any less lofty or rigid when it comes to compromising and finding a happy middle ground.

In Relationships: An intelligent partner does not always connote a thoughtful one, but in this instance, the INFJ mates do benefit from both. These personality types tend to use their broad intelligence, which includes being able to "read" people's emotions, to do kind, sweet, and affectionate things for those they love. Just don't cross your INFJ lover, because this type also has the brains to sniff out deceit and lies.

At Work: Having intelligence on the job is about more than just performing duties well. INFJs have an open dialogue with themselves, and they have the native intelligence to know when a job is for them or when it isn't. Because they are always seeking to do better for themselves and for the world around them, they may leave jobs if the career path doesn't seem to align with their ideals, their dreams, and their goals.

With Friends: If you need a dependable editor or someone to bounce an idea off of, the INFJ is your guy or gal. INFJs are nicely equipped with formidable intellects that are capable of understanding numerous subjects or fields of interest, and it makes knowing them — or better yet, being close friends with them — even better than if you were enjoying them solely for their personality. Plus, these Feeling types are happy to reach out and help in any way they can, even if it's a friend of a friend, or an acquaintance.

Health: INFJs have the smarts to become doctors themselves. But when it comes to their own health, while they can panic and get excessively worried, they do approach scares in an intelligent way: by gathering as much information as they can and weighing the validity of what they have learned. Plus, when they are the ones on the examination table, they are asking smart, informed questions, making the most of the precious little time patients tend to get with doctors.

Finance: Money matters really do matter, as they can affect every aspect of your life — and that gravitas is not lost on INFJs, who strive their whole lives to provide financial stability for themselves and their families. As far as they are concerned, it is simply smart, good sense to always have a paycheck coming in and to always make purchases that are well within one's budget. They might splurge from time to time on a nice vacation or a big TV, but you can bet they saved and crunched numbers beforehand.

33. Prone to Self-analysis

Positive: Always getting better — that's the slogan for any true INFJ, who is constantly examining him/herself to find ways that he/she can improve. INFJs' goals are dynamic, shifting to reflect the new possibilities that the they can see for themselves after a bout of self-reflection. It's a characteristic that places this personality type among the most admirable, because so many of us fail to meet our true potential. "Fail" is not a word in the INFJ vocabulary.

Negative: Self-analysis can, however, lead to self-doubt and self-degradation. Combined with the worried, fearful, and lonely characteristics that color the INFJ personality, turning inward for analysis can bring these types of individuals to a debilitating place where they end up getting frustrated or angry at themselves — and then take that negative energy and lash out at others in an uncharacteristic way, which can be truly frightening for their loved ones.

In Relationships: "How can I be a better partner to this person I love?" That's the question a self-analyzing INFJ asks him/herself when they are happily coupled off in a long-term relationship. Because INFJs are so picky when choosing their mates, finding one who actually meets their requisites can seem too good to be true, and so they want to do everything they can – including improving themselves, daily – to keep that person around.

At Work: Those employee evaluations are probably unnecessary for the INFJ, who has been evaluating him/herself since the moment he/she walked onto the job. But these INFJs are also assessing their happiness and their projected productivity in a given workplace, because living up to the personal goals and ideals that they have set is of the utmost importance — and those will change as they re-evaluate themselves concerning how far they have come and how far they feel they have yet to go.

With Friends: Being friends with INFJs can sometimes make you feel like crud — not because they have indicated through word or deed that you aren't good enough, but because they are always setting the bar so high for themselves, and you feel like an underachiever in comparison. What is important to note is that the INFJ loves his/her friends for exactly who they are, and wouldn't change a single thing, so this type's own personal self-analysis and accompanying quest for betterment is not a reflection on anyone else.

Health: INFJs like to keep a close eye on both their mental and physical health, so that if they wake up one morning and find that something isn't quite right, they can analyze that change, comparing it against previous days. This is good for them personally - so that coughs, bumps, or even extra weight that has accumulated receives its fair share of attention – as well as when they go to the doctor and are asked about the history of their symptoms or ailments.

Finance: "How can I be spending my money better?" the INFJ will ask him/herself. It's an important part of any adult's life, and few approach the topic with as much motivation as this personality type. If the INFJs feel as though they have spent too much on eating out, they will curb the tendency; or, if they are in their middle years and would like to have something to retire on, they might seek to better themselves by getting professional wealth-management help.

Book II.

Lives of Great INFJ's.

INFJs are a rare breed, and it's a shame because they are capable of so much! Then again, if there were more INFJs in the world, they might not seem quite as special and would end up even less appreciated than they already are. Some of the greatest people who have lived and done good works in this world were INFJs, including writers, civil leaders, and even acclaimed actors, so if you are an INFJ, you are in good company. If you know someone who is an INFJ or you suspect he or she might be, here is a quick run-down of the unique characteristics that make this personality type who they are.

Introverts are often misunderstood because while many of them are shy and retiring, plenty of them can be outgoing and outspoken! It's just that after they have their moment in the spotlight, they need to step away and be at peace, have time to collect their thoughts, and recharge their batteries. INFJs have the capacity to be leaders of entire nations, but they need their "me time" all the same, and many go to great lengths to ensure that they schedule those essential moments into their daily lives. Often, INFJs use those quiet, contemplative periods for some artistic endeavor, like writing or reading.

Intuitives are the dreamers who hope for a better tomorrow. While Thinking Intuitives tend to wonder, "What can I invent? How can I make this machine work better?" Feeling Intuitives like INFJs want to engender greater social harmony and better interpersonal relationships. To their thinking, if people can get along better, then the future will be much brighter. Intuitives like INFJs also tend to look at the big picture, rather than focus on smaller details, and they are comfortable thinking about abstract ideas and theoretical situations.

Feeling types are the do-gooders who often place the emotional needs of others before their own. Their focus is on how word and action makes others feel, and while making decisions based on a feeling can land them in trouble at times (for instance, acting on a rush of emotion rather than logically thinking through a problem can be dangerous), their hearts are almost always in the right place. Their compassion and empathy make them relatable and immediately likable.

Judging personalities have the innate ambition and drive to get things done in a timely and responsible manner. Perceivers tend to take their own meandering paths when it comes to their pursuits, both in their careers and personal lives, but Judging types are much more committed; their actions have a feeling of agency to them, which is why INFJs are so subtly formidable — they are underdogs, the secret weapons employed by those who recognize their strength and ambition.

Here are 13 great examples of some famous INFJs who have helped shape the course of history.

1. Geoffrey Chaucer

His Introvert Advantage: Geoffrey Chaucer was many things: a poet, a philosopher, and a diplomat, but he was, above all, a wit, and he had the ability to see things with his keen observer's eye. He might have had a silvery tongue (as anyone employed on overseas missions for the king must), but from the works he left us, it is obvious that, like an Introvert, he preferred to sit back and watch, take everything in, and consider, rather than jump into the action and put himself at the front. That he wrote at all is not necessarily an indication that he was an Introvert (as it never is), but the sheer volume of the works that Chaucer produced indicates that he was comfortable being closeted away for long periods of time, bent over his manuscripts. Chaucer held many different positions over his lifetime, working in quite a variety of fields, and it is suggested that he modeled many of his characters (especially those in *The Canterbury Tales*) after the people he met, a task that takes no small amount of time or concentration, especially when the characters are so brilliantly satirized.

His Intuitive Advantage: Like many Intuitives, Chaucer was gifted with languages, and he would not have been chosen for diplomatic ventures had he not been fluent in French, the standard language of the courts of Europe. Only those with an elite grasp of the language would be able to undertake translation work, as Chaucer did. While he worked at the court, there can be no doubt that he was kept busy, as Medieval kingdoms and politics were highly complex and inordinately inefficient, and he was in charge of overseeing the king's building projects for a time. Yet it is while he held this post that scholars attribute many of his writings, proving that Geoffrey Chaucer had that undeniable impulse to create and to imagine, two traits that every Intuitive can relate to. One can easily imagine him with his public face on, energetic and practical, then retiring to his chambers with candles all around him, gaining quiet energy as he made his words come to life, a great Prometheus at his forge, the urge to write as strong as the need to breathe.

His Feeling Advantage: Though it is disputed, historians and scholars generally agree that Chaucer's *The Book of the Duchess* was composed to commemorate the death of Blanche of Lancaster, the wife of John of Gaunt (one of the younger sons of the illustrious Edward III). Though she was a great heiress and the marriage was arranged, it appears to have been a happy one, and the two produced 10 children (7 of whom survived infancy). She died very young, only about 22 or 23, and there are indications that, though Gaunt married twice more after her death, he sincerely mourned her passing. Historians have suggested that *The Book of the Duchess*, which describes the mourning of a knight for his lady "White" (Blanche being a French-derived word for white), is certainly meant to honor her, perhaps for one of the special anniversary commemorations that Gaunt held each year, but it was also meant to coax this prince out of his grave sadness. A Feeling Chaucer seems to be suggesting that her death was indeed very tragic, but as even the lowliest peasant must do, so must a prince of England find the will to carry on.

His Judging Advantage: In a way, if it weren't for Chaucer's industriousness around the court, signs of his Judging nature, we would know significantly less about the author who left us the richly hilarious work, *The Canterbury Tales.* Since very few people from this time left any of their own written accounts of their lives (blogging hadn't quite taken off yet), we must rely on the legal and court documents which detail the activities of the king and courtiers. Thankfully, Chaucer was part of the busy environment, starting as a squire and working his way up to more illustrious positions — not bad for a kid whose family sold wine. That he was able to do so is an indication of both his intelligence and his ambition; one gets the sense that this was a guy who aimed high and took his chance when it was presented. Making tough decisions that turn out to be great decisions is something that successful Judging types do, and Chaucer is a fine example of that. Despite the fact that he lived through considerable political upheaval — the unfortunate reign of Richard II, who was deposed by his cousin, Henry IV — his ability to do the work that was asked of him with a sense of urgency and responsibility stood him in good stead and he never lost footing while the hands of government changed.

2. Gillian Anderson

Her Introvert Advantage: Gillian Anderson had rather inconspicuous beginnings. She was born into a family that moved to Puerto Rico from Chicago when she was only 15 months old, then moved on to England when she was about two. At the age of 11, Anderson returned with her family to the United States, where the kids of Grand Rapids, Michigan, picked her on for her English accent, so she quickly modified her speech to sound more American. She describes herself as a punk in her teen years, one of the few kids, let alone girls, who wore her hair in a Mohawk and donned a nose ring, and as the outside world stared, she withdrew further into herself, using isolation as armor. Her Introversion was further fostered by the claustrophobic work schedule she maintained while on set for *The X-Files*, her break-out TV show; she met her first husband and had a baby, and when she wasn't working, which wasn't often, she clung to those quiet, domestic moments where there was no one talking at her and she could just be, without distractions, and those are the types of Introverted moments that sustained her through nine years of the show.

Her Intuitive Advantage: When she was 24 and just starting *The X-Files*, Gillian Anderson had no clear picture of her future; she got word that she had nabbed the part on the day her last unemployment check arrived, so she was just happy to have a job and some income. Yet as her success grew more assured, she blossomed as an actress and began to take on a variety of different roles, seeing herself as more than just a TV FBI agent. One gets the sense that her Intuitive aspect grew and matured as she did, both in her years and in confidence. Despite her

INFJ: 33 Secrets From The Life of an INFJ

success, Gillian maintains her "weirdness," a clear indication that her creative juices are still flowing, and her desire to make sense out of chaos — as words on a page inevitably are, until we inject meaning and nuance into them — continues more powerfully than it has before. As an actress who has taken on a wealth of roles, from a *belle époque* beauty in *The House of Mirth* to the melodramatic Blanche DuBois in *A Streetcar Named Desire*, Gillian ably uses her body to interpret and emote.

Her Feeling Advantage: While actors and actresses clearly rely on the impetus of their own emotions, as well as those of their audience, to produce effective work, Gillian Anderson is also a devoted humanitarian who uses her celebrity to effect positive change in the world around her. Her activism is wide and varied, from speaking on behalf of the Neurofibromatosis Network (which is particularly dear to her heart because her brother was diagnosed with it and then died when he was only 31 years old), to making much of her support of PETA. She has been aligned with the LGBT community for years, and has also spoken out in favor of international women's rights. In her personal life Gillian Anderson has shown a strong desire to love and be loved, and she seeks out committed relationships; for her first child, she felt such a protective, motherly concern that she refused to let her daughter be photographed until the child was 7 years old.

Her Judging Advantage: Gillian Anderson has said that she considers herself to be controlling, but my, how far that "controlling" Judging nature has taken her. Though in her younger years she might have been considered more of a Perceiving type, age and maturity have done their work, and she is now a reliable and committed actress. Her lengthy body of work, as well as her numerous nominations (with a few impressive awards!), is a fine example of how ambitious and decisive this actress can be when it comes to choosing roles that will challenge her and offer her the opportunity to show range — range that extends far beyond the skeptical, tight-lipped Dana Scully. Though many writers can show the traits of a Perceiving type, Gillian Anderson has shown a surprising aptitude for the written word; it has been 15 years, and she is still doggedly adapting a novel about the children of a Holocaust survivor into a screenplay, which she also intends to one day direct. Whereas Perceivers would have given up and moved onto something else after 15 days or 15 weeks, this is only proof that Gillian Anderson wants to see things finished, and finished the right way.

3. Cate Blanchett

Her Introvert Advantage: When one of her directors commented, "She's a private person," he could not have described Cate Blanchett better. This screen siren, who is bound to remind us all of the icon from the Golden Age of Hollywood, has scooped up numerous awards (it's really not an award season unless she is nominated for something) and has earned a reputation for being one of the most brilliant actresses on the planet; yet aside from glossy magazine covers, you don't realize she's there until another one of her fabulous movies comes out. This is because Cate is essentially an Introvert, and though she can float down the red carpet looking like a goddess and call out a fashion show for blatant sexism ("Do you do that to the guys?" she asked, as the camera swept from her ankles upward), it is obvious that her need for privacy and isolation, far away from the paparazzi and the crowds of screaming fans, is a priority, both for herself and for her entire family, which consists of her husband, three boys, and one girl.

Her Intuitive Advantage: Truly, no one dazzles on screen the way Cate Blanchett does, and her ability to interpret lines and turn them into the utterings of real people who have real feelings and real motivations is astounding. This is particularly obvious in her range, as she has played a powerful elf from Middle Earth, Queen Elizabeth I, a narcissistic socialite who is suddenly stricken with hard financial times, a lost schoolteacher who commits adultery with a student...and the list goes on and on, and it's not just that she takes on these roles, but that her Intuitive aspect is so fine-tuned that she makes each and every one of them come utterly alive, to the point where you forget that you are watching an actress at her craft. Her vision for the arts is also apparent, as she served with her husband as co-CEO and artistic director for the Sydney Theater Company, a more administrative role that nonetheless required her to look ahead to the future of theater in Australia and make decisions about where the company was heading.

Her Feeling Advantage: Cate has been married since 1997, and it is interesting that she regards her husband as one of the few people she can discuss work with; she considers him to be the font of constructive criticism. Feeling types can have a very difficult time taking critique, but it is obvious that this emotional and professional woman found someone whose emotion and professionalism matched hers. Her compassion for the less fortunate was brought to light more tellingly in 2015, when it was confirmed that she and her husband, who already had three boys, decided to adopt a little girl. Cate cited the need to get children out of foster homes and into permanent families as part of her husband's and her desire to adopt, displaying immense empathy for the millions of children stuck in the foster care system. She has also shown support for causes that aim to improve the environment and provide clean drinking water to people have little-to-no access, and she has been an outspoken proponent for gender equality both around the world and in the arts.

Her Judging Advantage: One gets the distinct impression that in Hollywood there are a few different types of actors, and that Cate Blanchett belongs in the group with those who choose to behave with class, style, and graciousness. If she had gone into a professional career, she would be at the top of the company, the CEO — such are her administrative gifts and her ability to pay attention to details — but as an actress, she relays her stardom into projects that are greater than herself and require serious commitments of time and responsibility. Then there is her family life, which is so indicative of her Judging personality. She married her husband in 1997, and their only major blips have involved health issues, not fidelity problems. They have three boys, and adopted a little girl in 2015, and they moved back to their native Australia to be closer to family and have a deeper sense of connection with the country from which they came. None of this has had any impact on Cate's acting career, and indeed it seems as though her steady, secure private life has been an anchor for her glamorous, international acting career.

4. Nelson Mandela

His Introvert Advantage: Just because Introverts tend to be quieter, happier in the background, and less sociable than their Extraverted counterparts, we might assume that they are less capable of managing big matters and effecting great change. This is a deeply flawed logic that is refuted by Nelson Mandela, the first South African president and one of the most influential and courageous men to have walked the planet. His Introversion has been decided by the man himself, who described his own personality as "serious" and "observant," two traits that get thrown at Introverts quite a bit. Yet his Introversion opened the door to serious and intelligent political thought and deep introspection about who he was as a man and what he hoped to achieve. He was deeply influenced by his roots in the tribal community where he was raised, where the king would only speak after everyone else had spoken; throughout the gatherings, the man in charge did not lead the discussions, but instead let all else have their say, and as they talked and argued, he observed them — what they were saying, how they said it, and what was the measure of each man.

His Intuitive Advantage: It is hard to imagine that after 27 years in prison Nelson Mandela kept his dreams alive, but he did; his Intuitive nature did not simply up and vanish because of the conditions of his surroundings. He continued his journey toward what he knew would be a better tomorrow, even in his prison, even after contracting tuberculosis. He was able to complete a law degree remotely through the University of South Africa, and he worked in secret on an autobiography (which would be published after his release, in the year he became president). Is this the behavior of a man who has given up all hope of a future? Are these the actions of a man who has resigned himself and his country to a system of legal racism? It most certainly is not, and though Mandela's Intuitive aspect must have struggled throughout the years of incarceration to keep hope alive, it did prevail, so that when he was released, the first thing he did was urge foreign powers to continue their pressure on the South African government (which they had been doing in large part to urge the release of Mandela).

His Feeling Advantage: Called "Tata" or "father," Mandela is revered in South Africa as the father of the country. While he wanted to see blacks raised up to the same level as whites, he hoped to achieve this as peacefully as possible during his time as president, which is notable for its dismantling of apartheid. It seems that every moment he spent in jail, he was thinking about the welfare of the people who would eventually elect him to the highest position in the land. He once declared himself prepared to die for his ideals — he was therefore prepared to die for the idea that everyone should be treated equally and racism should not be tolerated, let alone sanctioned by the state. Compassion for people he did not know and had never met was one of the defining traits of Nelson Mandela, as it is one of the aspects of the Feeling function.

His Judging Advantage: INFJs are like the administrative, more responsible siblings to INFPs, and Mandela exemplified all that a committed, loyal, and reliable man should be. He not only stood up for his ideals, but he was also willing to put in the legwork necessary to see them brought to action, no matter how hard the current rushed in the other direction. That he refused release from his prison in exchange for desisting from armed opposition (he came to the conclusion reluctantly, after years of peaceful protest, that armed opposition was the only way to get his government to implement change), staying loyal to his beliefs, and to the trust that others had placed in him, without a moment's hesitation. Then he led the way for his country, shouldering the immense responsibility of running an entire nation that was still badly bruised from decades of hate and fearmongering, and he did it with humanity, warmth, and a strong sense of moral right.

5. Martin Luther King, Jr.

His Introvert Advantage: It might seem surprising that one of the most charismatic and moving public speakers to have ever lived was also an Introvert, but there is no denying that Martin Luther King, Jr. did was what necessary — indeed, what moved him in his heart — for the good of social change, yet he remained a private individual who kept his friends close and his family closer. A precocious student, once King applied himself to his studies, he showed immense promise as a scholar, entering college at the age of 15, graduating by 18, and earning his doctoral degree before he was 25. While he was phenomenally intelligent, it speaks to his gifts as an Introvert — gifts of observation and contemplation — that he was able to accelerate his studies at such a speed. Then there was his ability not just to lead, but also to listen — as an observer in a world that was changing fast, King opened his ears like an Introvert and heard people's suggestions and opinions.

His Intuitive Advantage: "I have a dream," King intoned in his most famous speech, and he could very well have followed that up with, "for I am an Intuitive" (but thankfully he didn't!). His Intuitive aspect shows in the work that he did and the vision that he strived for his entire life — the equality of all men and women in the world, regardless of skin color. There is no telling why some people can participate half heartedly in a cause while others make it their sole reason for drawing breath, but King was most certainly in the latter group, and he held onto his goal and his hope for a better tomorrow — indeed, he clung to it with the ferocity of a man thrown overboard with only a lifesaver. He was arrested 29 times for his willingness to be identified as part of the Civil Rights

Movement, and his speech at the 1963 March on Washington electrified the entire nation with its impassioned call for a country in which all stood on equal footing.

His Feeling Advantage: One of King's most astounding traits was the lengths to which he was prepared to go so that all of his brothers and sisters in love and unity could be part of a world which welcomed them equally — not segregated them. King lived out his adult life in the service of others, yet there is an equally fascinating Feeling personality who emerges out of what we know to be evidence that he participated in extramarital affairs. King was not a saint; he was a man as human and as flawed as any of us, and his deeply emotional behavior is an indication of how he could act without logic at times. Yet it in no way diminishes his powerful and positive influence on the course of American history; if anything, it makes him even more relatable to the rest of us "regular" people who feel as though we are too flawed to do good.

His Judging Advantage: King's Judging aspect seemed to articulate itself when he was a junior at Morehouse College and still just a teenager. Despite his youth, King's spiritual growth helped him mature and become the committed, devoted man and civil leader he would blossom into in his 20s and 30s. His thoughtful and contemplative nature allowed him to more fully articulate his feelings and opinions when it came to the forward motion of the Civil Rights Movement, but his Judging aspect imbued him with the extraordinary ambition and drive to see his ideals through to completion. Though he lived to see successes for his movement, there is no doubt that he was capable of much more, and were it not for his tragic assassination in 1968, America might be an even greater bastion of equality.

6. Mother Teresa

Her Introvert Advantage: Aside from all the good things that Mother Teresa did for people throughout her long life, one of her most significant contributions to this world was that she listened to people. Introverts have a bad rap for being shy or afraid to speak up, and they are sometimes underappreciated for their lack of spoken words. Yet just because Introverts aren't speaking, it doesn't automatically follow that they are not communicating. Many beautiful quotes have been attributed to Mother Teresa, but she was first and foremost an observer and a listener, a woman who preferred that her speech and her needs take a backseat to service for others and for her God. The world is a much better place because Mother Teresa chose to look around herself in the Introverted fashion and witness the poverty, illness, and social injustice that needed fixing.

Her Intuitive Advantage: Only a woman with such tremendous insight and hope for the future could place the rest of her life in the hands of the Catholic Church at the age of 18. That is precisely what Mother Teresa did, making her way toward Ireland (from her home in Albania) to join a religious order in Dublin, where she could learn English and then be sent as a missionary to India. Mother Teresa's belief — instilled in her from the time she was very young by her charitable mother — that service to others was the highest calling and the best way to change the world around her and lift people out of their poverty manifested itself in a religious calling, to which she remained faithful her entire life. Her idealistic hopes that she could effect change never left her, and indeed, it seemed to grow stronger as she matured.

Her Feeling Advantage: Mother Teresa was, in a way, the living embodiment of the Feeling aspect. Her every action from the time she was 18 was in service to others. With her incredible stores of compassion and empathy, she felt deeply the pain and suffering that others endured. While her own upbringing was not one of lavish wealth, she recognized how lucky she had been to receive a formal education, and it was soon after she arrived in India that she saw the truest and most desperate forms of poverty. Never one to let evil or injustice stand, she threw herself into her charitable works, learning Bengali and Hindu so that she could fluently communicate with the children of the Indian villages, eventually moving into the slums of Calcutta to aid the poor who lived and died there — people forgotten by everyone else, but not by Mother Teresa, who made it her life's mission to improve their quality of life.

Her Judging Advantage: It is interesting to note that when Christ spoke to Mother Teresa and told her to change her plans from teaching to simply "helping the poor," He didn't leave her with anything more concrete than that. It was this remarkable woman who transformed His word into the vast network of charitable organizations that became an international source of refuge and hope for the world's poor. She helped to establish schools, hospitals, orphanages, and shelters all around the world, and when AIDS became a new, terrifying epidemic the world over, she threw herself into the care of those who contracted and suffered with the disease. She did this with the devotion, commitment, and sense of responsibility that makes all Judging types capable of reaching out to others — from a place of vision and a sense of moral right — to better our little planet.

7. Mahatma Gandhi

His Introvert Advantage: In a way, Mahatma Gandhi was subjected to a life of introversion whether he liked it or not — he frequently spent long periods of time away from his family and conversed with friends by mail. But the Father of India was deeply Introverted in his own way, an observant individual who absorbed experiences and sights and then reflected on them, made sense of them, and gathered strength and energy in the process of articulating his thoughts and opinions. He found himself in the limelight on many occasions, but he never sought it for any reason other than to bring attention to his goals, preferring to do all that he could for his causes without thrusting himself forward for acclaim. He was a man who valued learning for its own sake, and he often immersed himself in the cultures of the people around whom he lived, and was willing to stop and hear out the opinions and philosophies of others.

His Intuitive Advantage: Though Gandhi urged others to act in the present and not worry about the future, he himself was quite concerned about the future for the sake of the people he represented. In his 21 years in South Africa, where he experienced, first hand, the racism and classism that plagued the country and particularly took aim at Indians who lived there, he saw even worse examples of injustice in the impoverished and beaten-down people who struggled to get through every day. When he finally returned to his native India, he took aim at the British government that had occupied India as part of its empire. With a great sense of destiny for the

Indian people, he worked tirelessly to gain Indian independence from Britain, as well as to level the playing field for all people, and gain more equal rights for women.

His Feeling Advantage: Though Gandhi was trained as a lawyer and obviously had a well-developed Thinking aspect that allowed him to act with thoughtful and logical analysis, his Feeling aspect provided the impetus to put those legal skills into practice for the greater good. Certainly his sharp intelligence and keen understanding of legal matters were a boon when he was facing off against an empire, but without his Feeling aspect, he might not have felt compelled to face off against anyone to begin with. For Gandhi, the fight was about justness, freedom and autonomy. Too long had his country been subjected to the rule of a foreign power that misused and abused the Indian people, and Gandhi translated his immense distaste for the British Empire's tyrannical rule into the tireless campaign for independence that was called "Quit India". Throughout his life and all of his social and political activities, he strongly advocated for non-violent protest because, as he put it, "An eye for an eye would soon make the whole world blind."

His Judging Advantage: Gandhi's magnificent ability to galvanize and to attain progress was not just because of his idealism. Aside from being well educated, he was thoughtful about how to approach each campaign and he displayed a talent for being a good organizer of both people and action. He was also incredibly disciplined, living simply, eating no meat, and sometimes eating nothing for weeks so that his fasts could have a more profound influence on the people he opposed. And he was never once heard to complain or whine; he did it all willingly, happily even, because once he committed himself to a cause, he was there to stay, present in mind, body, and spirit. He had the typical Judging patience, the ability to play the long game, and he never showed resentment for the fact that results couldn't be achieved any faster than they were. Moreover, as a parent does for his child, Gandhi never gave up on his people. No wonder they called him "father"!

8. Eleanor Roosevelt

Her Introvert Advantage: Eleanor Roosevelt was born into a wealthy and recognizable family — her uncle, Teddy, gave her away at her wedding while he was sitting president — yet her childhood was as distant and unhappy as one could imagine. Naturally, a cold childhood does not an Introvert make, but it did leave this eventual First Lady with the impression that she could not rely on others for happiness, and if she wanted to get anything done in the face of opposition, she would have to summon her courage and do it, naysayers be damned. Though she was well liked and charmingly outspoken, Eleanor nonetheless kept close to herself, ensuring that her private life and inner emotions stayed private — and for good reason. Letters written between Eleanor and a Washington, D.C., journalist named Lorena Hickok hint strongly at a lesbian relationship; what would be scandalous today would have been unspeakably damaging to her and her husband's reputations back then.

Her Intuitive Advantage: When Franklin Delano Roosevelt came home from a long trip, his wife Eleanor did the wifely thing: she put his tired bones to bed and then set about unpacking his luggage. What she found in his suitcase changed the tenor of their relationship as we know it. Letters that proved he was in love with a younger woman were contained therein, but instead of folding with misery under the discovery, Eleanor took advantage of her position of power (a gentle threat of divorce was enough to make him come to his senses) and ferried his marital failings into her political future. This was in 1918, and by the time FDR had achieved the heights of his ambitions — becoming president — his First Lady had an equally ambitious vision for what her position in the White House would encompass. She had gone from shrinking violet under her mother-in-law's iron rule to independent and visionary political and social activist with a voice that was all her own.

Her Feeling Advantage: Eleanor had the great fortune to be married to a man who, once he realized what an asset she was, encouraged and supported her political and social activities while he was president. In turn, the country was made a better place because Eleanor worked with impressive ambition to improve the situation of America's women and children, to bring about greater civil justice for blacks, to advocate on behalf of the poor and to show her support for the troops during World War II. On the one hand, it greatly enhanced her own prestige and the public support of her husband, but on the other, this was a genuinely independent-thinking woman who wanted to use her position of great importance — and her unique access to the most powerful man in the world — to help others less fortunate. With her great Intuitive aspect paired with her Feeling function, Eleanor Roosevelt realized that by strengthening the weak, the entire country grew stronger as a whole.

Her Judging Advantage: With her keen political mind and no-nonsense attitude, First Lady Eleanor Roosevelt exemplified the virtues of the Judging type. She planned and put into action many different initiatives, programs and personal ventures, whether it was traveling to meet and speak with the poor and hear their stories, making public speaking engagements so that people could come out and see their First Lady (the fees almost all went to charity), or writing a syndicated newspaper column called "My Day" — which gave her readers the unprecedented feeling that she was right there with them, offering her ideas and thoughts. She was organized, she was galvanized and, perhaps surprisingly, after discovering her husband's letters from another woman, she was a devoted wife to her polio-stricken husband, choosing to move past the hurt and throw her focus and ambition into working with him to carve out a better, more just America.

9. Carl Jung

His Introvert Advantage: Carl Jung, one of the pioneers of modern psychiatry and the man who formed the personality theory upon which Isabel Briggs Myers based the MBTI system, was an obvious Introvert from a very young age. Socially awkward and not good at making friends, he even started faking illness in order to stay home from school and further isolate himself from others. Though in childhood this was rather unfortunate (as it is for lots of Introverts), as an adult it manifested itself in much more constructive ways, making Jung noticeably serious, contemplative, observant, and willing to invest hours into involved, deep discussions with close associates (like Freud), in readings of lengthy and complex tomes for greater understanding of his field, and in writing his own books, which he published right up to his death.

His Intuitive Advantage: Intuitives don't mind getting their hands dirty with the less-than-concrete — unlike Sensing types, hard facts are less desirable than possibilities and theories, and Jung played around with this perspective throughout his entire career. Intuitives are known as interpreters, and while some may use this to their advantage and acquire a new language (or two), Jung was interested in dream interpretation — what our subconscious is telling us while we sleep. But he was also a proponent of art therapy, using the creation of art to alleviate stress and depression and to explore the hidden depths of an individual. He himself turned to art for this reason, showing the Intuitive impulse for creativity as a means to express something that cannot be put into words. Ultimately, Jung provided an innovative way of looking at psychology, introducing or expanding on ideas that might not receive the attention they do today if he had not paved the way.

His Feeling Advantage: There has been some debate over whether or not Carl Jung was an INFJ. There is some sentiment that he might have been an INTJ, the master architect. While it's true that Jung undertook no great charitable words and his passions were rather ordinary, his emphasis on the spiritual and metaphysical make a strong argument for his being a Feeling type rather than a Thinking type. For instance, rather than advocate a strict dietary regimen or exercise schedule, Jung suggested that one of the ways alcoholics cope with abstaining is through spirituality. He was personally interested in many different types of religions and religious philosophies, and he theorized that only through spirituality could an individual be truly happy. That he was concerned at all with happiness — over, say, usefulness or efficiency — indicates Jung's preference for Feeling (although he clearly had a well-defined Thinking aspect that was used to great effect).

His Judging Advantage: Carl Jung was a social scientist, and as a successful professional whose work has withstood many decades without any large-scale debunking (scientists will always squabble and debate, but there is no denying his influence), he has proven to be detail oriented and ambitious about his life's work. His writing is so full of nuance and complexity that it would be hard to believe a Perceiving type could dedicate such a large part of his life to committing all of these ideas to paper, let alone keep up the relentless correspondence that Jung did with the great thinkers of his day. Jung met life with a seriousness that is both Introverted and Judging, showing a solitary dedication for a field that he didn't even think about entering when he first matriculated at university, but that captivated him after he discovered its dual emphasis on both body and mind.

10. Florence Nightingale

Her Introvert Advantage: Insightful and serene even in the face of the bloodiest chaos, Florence Nightingale in her youth was described as being awkward in social situations and, like a true Introvert, she loathed being the center of attention, something that must have vexed her mother, who fancied herself a socialite. A graceful youth, Florence was a lovely young woman, but despite her physical charms she preferred not to thrust herself forward and seek the limelight. Indeed, her attention from the start was captured by the sick and the impoverished, and she knew from a young age what she wanted to do with her life. Like many an Introvert, Florence — who was named after the city in Italy where she was born to wealthy, upper-class parents — held her dreams close and only showed her hand when it was absolutely necessary. Then, she clung to her desires with a stubbornness that shocked her parents, who forbade her from pursuing a career — scandalous in the first place — in nursing, of all practices.

Her Intuitive Advantage: Nursing is like a religious calling: it is a vocation, and it is not to be taken lightly. One must feel it deep down inside one's very being, from a place that cannot be described or articulated. This is what Florence felt as a child who helped to care for the sick and poor people near her ancestral home in England. It was a feeling beyond fact or evidence, and it was likely that her Intuitive aspect is what made sense of the urge and gave her the ability to understand what her path in life must be. Florence displayed other apparent Intuitive traits as well, such as her gift for languages — she studied French, Italian and German, in addition to her native English. Her writing shows a flair for description, melding her knowledge of classical literature with her own bright, thirsty mind. And though she was a Victorian woman, born into a wealthy family that expected her to marry and produce children, Florence always had that Intuitive sense that she was destined for much more.

Her Feeling Advantage: There are few people in this world who have done as much as Florence Nightingale to help our sick and our poor, and it all stems from her natural compassion and empathy toward people who were born with much, much less than she. Sometimes "causes" can be fashionable, such as the modern-day "green" movement and the organics sections that have cropped up in all of our supermarkets, but that most certainly was not the case in the 19th century. While caring for the poor on a superficial level was considered good breeding by a lady of means (distributing alms, sewing linens, and even visiting sick villagers), actually tending to them as a career, rather than as an item on one's to-do list, was not a stylish trend, and Florence's Feeling aspect was therefore sincere, an innate part of who she was and the driving force behind the actions that would lead her to become the beloved Lady of the Lamp, and perhaps the most famous nurse who ever lived.

Her Judging Advantage: Florence Nightingale wasn't just a nurse — she utterly changed and redefined the concept of nursing as a career. This is where her Judging aspect is most obvious; when she was sent to administer care to the soldiers of the Crimean War, while acting as manager of the corps of nurses, she managed to turn around the horrific conditions the women discovered when they arrived at Istanbul. Her first course of action was to effectively shame the British government, by way of a public letter to the London Times, into providing better facilities and medical equipment for the wounded and sick. Thereafter, her committed and continuous advocacy on behalf of the soldiers in Crimea helped to reduce the death rate to 1/10th of what it had been before she arrived. And she didn't stop there; for the rest of her life, Florence Nightingale was a proponent for an organized, trained nursing system, and her book, *Notes on Nursing*, which was culled from her experiences and insights, is still read by new nursing students today.

11. Jimmy Carter

His Introvert Advantage: One might think that in order to be the leader of the free world, an Extraverted personality is an absolute necessity. One might think wrong. Look at Jimmy Carter, the 39th president of the United States, and an Introvert through and through. He is actually an exemplary Introvert, as he embodies the true spirit of the aspect. He is capable without being flashy, commanding but not overwhelming or "in your face," and an able communicator thanks to his introspective nature, which keeps him from blurting out the first thing that crosses his mind. While he has been described as shy, there is no doubting that when the matter at hand is one that has his full attention, he can be as forceful and purposeful as any Extravert, if not more so because he has taken the time to thoroughly consider the matter before resting on a decision.

His Intuitive Advantage: Like many great men, Jimmy Carter had an idea of how the country should be. But before he took on Washington, he worked hard as governor in his own state of Georgia, improving the efficiency of the government there and working to expand the opportunities for poor people and people of color. He showed incredible vision in all of his changes, especially in a state deeply entrenched in the South, where the vestiges of the *"Gone with the Wind"* era were still visible. He took his dreams and his ideals to the White House in 1977, and there he added two of the most important departments to our nation's future: the Department of Education and the Department of Energy. He was deeply forward thinking, Intuitive in his belief — far ahead of his time

— that the way to a better tomorrow in America was through the education of its young people and the proper harnessing and usage of energies.

His Feeling Advantage: Carter had a special reason to champion the causes of the poor in America: when his family farm fell on hard times after the death of his father, he and his wife, and their family, were forced to rely on government-subsidized housing. Though he was a humble man to begin with, this experience gave him a personal taste of what life was like for the impoverished, and he never forgot that. His governance and presidency were filled with nods specifically to African Americans, poor people, and others who suffered from oppression. In his post-presidential years, Carter has been a champion of human rights all around the globe, and in 2002 this undeniably Feeling man won the Nobel Peace Prize for his tireless work in finding peaceable solutions to the crises that inflict unspeakable horrors on people all around the globe.

His Judging Advantage: Carter has always funneled his energies through his Judging aspect, so that when he sets out to do something, he does it with great thoughtfulness, attention to detail, and organization, so that his endeavors are less likely to fail from the outset. His Judging aspect is, at times, what gives him such steely ambition and unwillingness to back down from the things he truly believes in. Interestingly enough, the Judging part of his personality can be seen in his handling of the gubernatorial race in Georgia in the 1970. Here, he played the long game, displaying the patience that only a Judging type can summon. To woo voters, he gave the appearance of dropping his civil rights platform entirely, a strategy that must have been excruciating; yet once he won, he resumed his previous efforts on behalf of the African-American population, much to the consternation of the pro-segregation voters he won.

12. Mary Wollstonecraft

Her Introvert Advantage: Brilliantly intellectual and astonishingly passionate, Mary Wollstonecraft is perhaps best known for birthing the novelist who penned *Frankenstein*, Mary Wollstonecraft Shelley, yet she was an entirely gifted and forward-thinking woman in her own right. Throughout her life, she formed intense attachments with her friends, focusing much of her attention on them (in one instance, even leaving the school she had founded to help nurse a woman in Lisbon, Portugal). Though she was good company, her preference for the inner world inside her mind was obvious — she was a prolific writer, both professionally as an author and personally, as a diarist. In a way, she had to turn inward because the ideas that she had were so scandalous that when her widower published her biography, her reputation was blackened for a century.

Her Intuitive Advantage: Intuitives live in a world beyond the physical: a mental, intellectual, and emotional plane where ideas reign supreme. Unorthodox and unconventional Mary Wollstonecraft might not have outwardly defied the norms of 18th-century England, but her mind was practically swarming with ideas that could have gotten her imprisoned. Though she married and produced children like a good Georgian woman should, inside she was fiery, open-minded, and untraditional. Her creative impulses compelled her to write, and though she only did so for a brief time (she died when she was just 38 years old), her work reveals the innermost thoughts of a woman trapped by time and space, but yearning for a more perfect tomorrow. That tomorrow entailed a world where men and women lived side by side in equality; she blamed the dominant patriarchal society for making women weak when, if they were free, they could become just as strong and smart as any man.

Her Feeling Advantage: Mary grew up in a tumultuous household, with a father who wasted his money on doomed ventures and then drank himself into a rage, beating Mary's mother. Though her work describes a keen logic, it is experiences like these — raw, emotional — that ultimately made it impossible for her not to take up the pen and ink and put her incredibly rebellious thoughts to paper. She imagined a world where no little girl would have to sleep across the doorway of her mother's bedroom to protect her from an inebriated, violent father; she wrote so that, in her dream of dreams, her words might inspire a movement that would bring about a society where a wife who left her husband would not be shunned by society and forced to work in the only conditions afforded to women who deserted — soul-crushing labor in extreme poverty.

Her Judging Advantage: Though she spent a lot of her life drifting in the way you might expect from a Perceiver, Mary was quite motivated and clearly hoped to achieve a well-ordered (if not traditional) life. One example is her marriage to William Godwin, a fellow writer by whom she became pregnant; though she had been pregnant and given birth before, that lover left her. This one, however, promised her that if they married, though it was for the sake of societal decency, he would consider her his equal in every way. Before the marriage, though, Mary actually managed to support herself — by using her God-given literary talents! — at the offices of a new journal that her friend had started. It was a partnership that would last a decade, and Mary continued to show her commitment by writing articles up until her death.

13. Lady Gaga

Her Introvert Advantage: Though Lady Gaga is today the "Mother Monster" to millions of fans all around the world, as a youngster, she was just as inconspicuous as the rest of us, albeit with an obvious gift for music. Her descriptions of her childhood are quite normal, but like the Introvert that she is, there were always parts of her life that she kept separate from school friends and that separated her from them. Her intense passion for music meant that she would have to spend hours on her own practicing both piano and voice, and she even enrolled in acting classes. While there are a great many children in the world who participate in extracurriculars like band and choir, Lady Gaga knew from a young age that she both wanted and needed music on a different plane than most other people.

Her Intuitive Advantage: Lady Gaga's Intuitive aspect has helped her carve out a career in a number of ways. First, Intuitives are known for their creativity and their ability to understand and interpret the abstract. For some, that is language, but it can often manifest itself in music, both performing and writing — and Lady Gaga does both. Second, despite her glorious vocal talents, Lady Gaga has made a name for herself by shocking the heck out of everyone with her wild outfits and challenging music videos. Never one to blend in or do what everyone else is doing, Lady Gaga's extraordinarily imaginative mind has collaborated with other artistic sorts to create some of the most powerful and jaw-dropping images out there, whether it's photos of her walking a red carpet in a meat dress, or her depiction of Jesus and Judas as members of a biker gang.

Her Feeling Advantage: Early on in her career, Lady Gaga established herself as a voice for the "weird." There is an epidemic of bullying, where children are taking their own lives because they are picked on or perceive themselves as not "fitting in." Lady Gaga has always been outspoken in her appeal to everyone who feels marginalized, ignored, or even ostracized, and her message is one of compassion and empathy. She has reached out to the world and used her incredible influence to let people of all ages, races, sizes, shapes, orientations, etc. know that they don't have to change for anyone — they are the way they are because that is how they should be. Gaga has also helped to raise millions for different causes, such as disaster relief (particularly in Haiti and Japan) and HIV/AIDS research.

Her Judging Advantage: While Gaga might seem like she's a little bit off-kilter, don't let the stage presence fool you. This is one motivated, disciplined, and tough woman, and she has worked hard for her success. As mentioned, when she was just a child, not even a teenager, her ambitions were well defined, and she was taking classes that would stand her in good stead as an adult — dancing, singing, and acting. While her Intuitive idealism might have dreamed of making it big and changing the very genre of pop music, her Judging aspect is what put those dreams into reality, and she has continued to challenge herself and show her range, from a collaboration with Tony Bennett to singing the "The Hills are Alive" at the 2015 Oscars to great acclaim. Whatever Gaga is doing, she is making it look effortless. But the fact is that this Judging personality is a perfectionist who wants to get it right, down to the tiniest detail.

Printed in Great Britain
by Amazon